Presented

To _____

By _____

Date _____

Your
Tongue
Determines Your
Destiny

April Shenandoah

Your Tongue Determines Your Destiny
Copyright © 2012 by April Shenandoah
Revised printing 2015
ISBN 978-160683-421-3

15 14 13   6 5 4 3 2

Harrison House Publishers
P.O. Box 35035
Tulsa, OK 74145

Presentation graphic reprinted from *King James, Illustrated Bible,* World Publishers, Copyright 1954.
Library of Congress Cataloging-in-Publication Data
ISBN 978-0-9666517-1-3

Contents

Dedication
Memoriam

My precious grandparents/parents Lester Faye Hilborn and Mary (Mayme) Alta Nable Hilborn, were the light of my life. They raised me in a loving Christian home, teaching me by being a godly example to follow. Grandpap was my confidant and best friend. Gramy was the wisest person I've ever known and is still my greatest inspiration. Their WORDS framed my world!

1891-1966   1891-1982

Acknowledgments

Charles Capps— I know that I speak for many when I say "thank you" for writing *THE TONGUE—A Creative Force!* The truth embedded in every page took me to a new level of FAITH, and gave me a greater understanding of the POWER of the SPOKEN WORD! I'm still soaking-it-up. Your words of encouragement for *Your Tongue Determines Your Destiny* have been the highlight of this work.

Victor Chartrand— thank you for the many years of faithful support, for believing in me and all that I do. Your "scientific research" rubbed off on me. I now revel in acquired knowledge obtained from "researching," knowing that it improves every project and aspect of life.

Rudy Milanovich— you are the best! The many hats of expertise you wear amazes me! Thank you for your time and patience in helping me put this book together. Your calm spirit makes working with you a pleasure.

Michael Heyden— your threshold of patience is appreciated beyond words. Thank you for listening, my friend, even when you hear my ideas over and over. Your 25 years of support for me and the ministry, have helped me to keep-on, keepin'-on.

Jerry and Gail Nordskog— your caring hearts and your love for God and country are an example to follow! I treasure your friendship—as well as your Nordskog Publishing tips! Many thanks for giving me a deal I couldn't refuse, while completing this book at your writers-retreat-on-the-lake.

Jo-Anna Steely— this is a big thank you for everything that you have ever done for me that I may have failed to acknowledge. THANK YOU! Every time you encourage me and my work, I know I'm on the right track. I'm looking for the day that I see my name in your book—start writing Sis!

To Harrison House— I am honored to have *Your Tongue Determines Your Destiny* added to your outstanding collection of published works.

Gary Cole— where do I send the flowers? You were an angel in waiting with the assignment of carrying this book to its published destination! I will never forget your kindness!

Joyce Wormell— you are appreciated! I've learned that there is no need for me to be anxious during the editing process. Your thorough and brave editing taught me better sentence structure and how to eliminate the unnecessary. Thanks for the education!

Julie Werner— my dear Managing Editor...each time I received an e-mail from you I got excited—you always brought me good news. THANK YOU for allowing me to share my vision and opinions throughout this process.

Chris Ophus— I was told your cover designs are awesome—I say BRILLIANT! This cover is perfection!

Thank you to the entire Harrison House team that touched this book in any way!

Endorsements

The beloved psalmist David, who pursued and won the heart of God, said; *"Set a watch, O Lord, before my mouth; keep the door of my lips"* (Psalm 141:3).

More than a decade ago during the most severe trial of my life, my mother sent me the book *The Tongue: A Creative Force* by Charles Capps. That book renewed my hope and reset my destiny. The premise therein was the power of one's spoken confession based upon the author's faith in the Word of God. Until now, I have read that book fourteen times. Next to the Bible it has been the single greatest influence in my walk with Christ.

Because of the dramatic effect that book had upon me, since then, my interest in this subject has only increased. Subsequently, I have continued to research and read every thing available relative to this revelation.

April Shenandoah has proceeded to use her unique literary gift to address this issue, not mimicking the works of others, quoting clichés and playing it safe, but continuing where others leave off. I am sure you will be blessed and spiritually empowered when you finish her presentation that further pursues a matter that is exceeded only in importance by one's personal salvation. When you are finished, remember, I told you so.

-Bishop Samuel L. Smith
General Chairman, Apostolic World Christian Fellowship
Evansville, Indiana

I have found April Shenandoah's latest book to be a fascinating, spiritual, helpful read. It will receive a prominent place in my library, as I intend to read it again and again. It's a reminder of how vital our words are in creating our personal world. Believe me; April has done God's work with Your Tongue Determines Your Destiny. This book should be in every home. April has really done it!

-Gavin MacLeod
Actor/Spokesperson
Rancho Mirage, California

April Shenandoah is a woman of exceptional integrity and talent. She's a prolific writer and a good friend, whom I have known for many years. But most importantly, she is a woman with faith in her God and His Word. Through her own experiences she has learned, first-hand, the power and truth of God's spoken word. When spoken in faith, it is like a soothing salve that heals all it is applied to.

April has reminded us that we are all diseased in one way or another, in our thinking, our emotions, or our bodies. But, God has provided healing for it all. What we think and feel leads to what we say, and what we say is what we get.

-Tom D'Muhala
Nuclear Scientist: Former President of the Shroud of
Turin Research Project (USA & Italy)
Raleigh, North Carolina

April Shenandoah tells a simple truth we can all agree upon: When you think positive thoughts, speak positive words, and enact positive deeds, you will naturally manifest positivity in your life!

-Sara O'Meara
Co-founder of Child Help USA,
Founder of the Little Chapel
Scottsdale, Arizona

KWITCHURBELYAKIN is a word that was used when I was growing up, I just did not know how to spell it. April Shenandoah nails a subject that is spoken of in scripture that is abused on a daily basis, and like a tsunami, leaves many spiritual and mental bodies in its wake. That scripture is Proverbs 18:21, *"Death and life are in the power of the tongue."* These insights can help preachers bear witness to the truth about a subject that can either heal or hurt, bless or curse. Some families suffer from generational curses from tongues that continue to carve the next generation to pieces, as that next generation grows up to be like their teacher. This book contains great insights in giving life to families and relationships, especially with God.

April speaks of the blessing aspect of the tongue that can produce life, "unwavering faith is a God-given gift—a gift for the asking." Listening to the insights of April as she uses Scripture with real life examples is a blessing to all. They should put this book into their arsenal to help take them and their families into eternity, first by making it a part of their individual life, and then by sharing this gift with others. Thank you, April, for your efforts to address a subject that can make many people uncomfortable, in a way that when received, can help them and others around them grow.

-Dr. Gregory Thompson/Friend to Jesus
Founder of ASLEEP kNOw MORE
Humansville, Missouri

We have had the privilege of knowing and watching the spiritual growth of April Shenandoah for many years. For that reason and becauseof the courage she is showing in sharing that learning with the world, we are pleased to endorse Your Tongue Determines Your Destiny.

This book is packed with the Word of God success strategies you can start using and obtaining results immediately.

-Dr. Randy C. Brodhagen

Glory to God Ministries, International

Palm Springs, California

Foreword

April Shenandoah's book *Your Tongue Determines Your Destiny* is a very timely book for this generation. This book reveals how to construct your future by giving voice to God's Word on a daily basis. It also gives insight into how you can prosper and be in good health in perilous times. What you say is what you eventually get—good, bad or indifferent. So as she would say, *"Kwit Chur Bely Akin."*

As the Apostle Paul said, the Word is near you, in your mouth and then in your heart. Whose words are you using to map your future? April's book presents valuable information that is based on the authority of God's Word. It is also full of good news (Gospel) that is capable of changing your life forever. April presents the power of God's Word and how to use it to overcome the problems you face in life. She is a great communicator and says it in a way that is so easy to understand, you would have to have someone to help you misunderstand it.

So *READ IT, DO IT AND BE BLESSED!*

Charles Capps
Charles Capps Ministries, Inc.
England, Arkansas

Introduction

My grandparents, who are now with the Lord, adopted me when I was a very young child. Growing up in the Hilborn household was a positive experience. By their example I developed a strong constitution—spiritually, physically, and emotionally. I learned that it doesn't do any good to whine about anything! Gramy would sometimes jokingly say, "Kwitchurbelyakin." A wooden sign saying just that hung on the wall of our kitchen. It was a great conversation piece for visitors trying to figure out what it said. That impressionable, strangely spelled word that was in view for every meal translates—*QUIT YOUR BELLY ACHING!*

As I learned about the power of the spoken word, it became clear that we as believers are not practicing one of the most basic Biblical principles—ask, believe, and receive. We are to say what we want, and expect it! The trick is to know what we want—not being wishy-washy.

About 15 years ago, I decided I wanted a conversion van. Every time I saw one on the highway I would say, "That's the one I want God—a white high-top, with a TV and a VCR." I did that for several months, and one fine day that white high-top van was miraculously mine. That's the short version of my "Miracle Van" story (find the full story in chapter 2). That's one example of speaking and receiving from Daddy God. I didn't try to figure out how I could get the van or how I could afford it—I rested in the fact that God would supply it. When we know what we want—we can have it!

Ignorance, rebellion, and lack of (God's) knowledge will hold us back from receiving and progressing in life. Most of us take a lot of lumps that could have been avoided. You've heard it said that, "You are what you eat." Well...I'm here to tell you that "You are what you speak."

Boldly I say to you that this book can change your life. When you practice God's principles set forth herein, you will learn to walk in the POWER and AUTHORITY that Jesus tells us we have. Get excited! The WORDS in this book will reveal how to move mountains and produce your heart's desires—by the very WORDS that roll off of your tongue!

In the Beginning...

...God created the heavens and the earth by SPEAKING them into existence!

"God said, Let there be light: and there was light." (Genesis 1: 3)

The first book of the Bible tells us the order in which God spoke His creation into being.

"**And God said,** Let there be a firmament in the midst of the waters, and let it divide the waters from the waters" (verse 6).

"**And God said,** Let the waters under the heaven be gathered together unto one place, and let the dry land appear: and it was so" (verse 9).

"**And God said,** Let the earth bring forth grass, the herb yielding seed, and the fruit tree..." (verse 11).

"**And God said,** Let there be lights in the firmament of the heaven to divide the day from night... for seasons, and for days and years" (verse 14).

The earth functions today, just as it did when it was set in motion in the beginning, when God said, "Let us make man in our image, after our likeness: and let them have dominion over the fish of the sea, and over the fowl of the air, and over the cattle, and over all the earth, and over every creeping thing that creepeth upon the earth" (verse 26). God's spoken Word brought about everything that mankind would need to sustain life on this planet. The power of the spoken Word started with the Creator of the universe. You are created in His image and your words have the same power! Words are the most powerful thing in the universe! Spoken words never return void. Your life mirrors what you speak—producing fruit after its own kind—whether it's rotten or sweet.

"In the beginning was the Word, and the Word was with God, and the Word was God" (John 1:1).

"It is written, man shall not live by bread alone, but by every Word that proceedeth out of the mouth of God." (Matthew 4:4)

Your Tongue Determines Your Destiny

What you say is what you get! The words that come out of your mouth chart the course for your life. James 3: 4-5 compares the tongue to a rudder of a ship. The rudder directs the course of the ship in the same manner as the tongue directs the course of your life. Throughout the Bible, God plainly reveals that, "Death and life are in the power of the tongue" (Proverbs 18:21). The words that you speak determine your destiny, as much as your thoughts. Your thoughts and words go hand-in-hand and must be in harmony in order to achieve your dreams.

Positive thoughts lead to positive words, while negative thoughts lead to negative words. However, if you have a positive thought but then think or say something negative concerning that thought, you will cancel out the positive from taking effect. If you are not automatically a positive person, then you will have to make an effort to change your thoughts and your words. When you truly grasp the fact that your words are "power in action," then you will be on your way to changing your life for the better.

The Words You Speak Today Will Be
the Life You Live Tomorrow

When I counsel with people and listen to them talk about their problems, it is evident why their situations never seem to change. Their thought patterns, along with the words they speak, are causing them to live a defeated life. People put themselves in bondage by their words. If you speak negative words, then you will have negative results. For instance, if you say that you get a cold every winter, you can't pay your bills, or you can't lose weight, then you will get a cold every winter, you won't be able to pay your bills, and you won't lose weight. However, you can also reverse your situation by changing your words. Eliminate negative words from your vocabulary. Refuse to get a cold and forbid any disease to come upon your body, in the name of Jesus. Thank God in advance for providing for you and your family financially. Make the decision to lose weight and say, "I'm losing weight now, everyday I'm losing more and more weight."

Each person's challenge is different. Some may have a great job, but are not successful in relationships—while others may have great relationships, but struggle financially. There are also people who never get sick, while others are always running to a doctor. God wants us whole in every area of our lives. Find and speak scriptures that pertain to your situation.

Life is not trouble-free; however, we have been given the POWER and AUTHORITY in the name of Jesus to be overcomers (1 John 5:4). Problems are very real, but they are only temporary. As Scripture says, ".... for the things which are seen are temporal; but the things which are not seen are eternal" (II Corinthians 4:18). The Holy Spirit often reminds us to walk in the POWER and AUTHORITY that God has given us. It is not my power or your power—it's God's power. It is in the name of His Son, Jesus, that gives us power. We are endued with His power from on high. He gave us the power and authority to"...call those things that aren't as if they are" (Romans 4:17).

As you read this book ask yourself, "Do I want to be pitiful or powerful?" God gave us His Living Word, which, when put into motion by our mouth, brings victory. Faith-filled words will put you over. When we confess God's Word and do not doubt in our heart, it produces overcoming power. What we speak will manifest in our lives. It is GOD'S GUARANTEE! Jesus said, "What things soever ye desire, when ye pray, believe that ye receive them, and ye shall have them" (Mark 11:24). Jesus said, "I will give unto thee the keys of the kingdom of heaven: and whatsoever thou shalt bind on earth, shall be bound in heaven: and whatsoever thou shalt loose on earth shall be loosed in heaven" (Matthew 16:19).

Unfortunately, people are binding the very things that they are praying about by giving the devil credit for their situations. Victory is hindered when you say that the devil is keeping you down. He will come in like a flood and bombard your mind with doubt and fear—keeping you down. The mind is the devil's playground! The devil says, "You will never amount to anything," God says, "You can do all things through Christ who strengthens you" (Philippians 4:13). The devil says, "You'll never have enough money,"God says, "There is no lack, for my God supplieth all of your need according to his riches in glory by Christ Jesus" (Philippians 4:19). The devil says, "You will never be healed," but the Word of God says, "By His stripes you were healed," (I Peter 2:24) and "He took our pains and carried our sicknesses" (Matthew 8:17).

The words we speak concerning our lives are taken literally by our computer-like brains. The words that we speak to others also leave their indelible mark. A few years ago while I was visiting the Union Rescue Mission in Los Angeles, I heard a woman speaker say, "When I was a child my father constantly told me I looked like a monkey."Of course her father loved her and was only joking, but she grew up believing that she was ugly because the daddy, whom she loved and trusted, told her this by saying that she looked like a monkey. As crazy as this sounds, she actually believed that she looked like a monkey. This shows the power that our words can have on others. Fortunately,God later delivered her from this false impression of herself.

Well-meaning words from family and friends can boost our self-image or stifle it. When I was 18, I was getting ready to take Hollywood by storm. Then someone asked me, "How long are you willing to struggle before you give up?" I answered, "Until I'm fifty." Do you see how that response set me up to fail? I told myself that I would struggle until I was 50 years old. At the time, however, I didn't know enough to respond by saying, "I will not struggle and I will not give up: I will succeed!"Although I dabbled in show business most of my life, I never made my total living in the field of entertainment because my mind had already been programmed with the outcome. As my words predicted, I gave up the dream at 50.

In Charles Capps' book *The Tongue—A Creative Force,* he reminds us that God said,"I have told My people they can have what they say, but My people are saying what they have." Really hear this! As long as you say what you have, you will continue to have what you say! Your words will produce no more, or no less, than what you say. Start listening to yourself talk. You will be amazed when you hear what is coming out of your mouth. Program yourself to proclaim those things that aren't as if they are, speak it and believe that "it" will come to pass.

A dear friend of mine who was unhappy about the way his life turned out, would often talk about suicide. He would ask, "What are you going to do when I'm gone?" At times, he would put his finger to his head gun-style, and pretend he was shooting himself. After a few years of this, he did just that—only this time the gun and bullets were real. Ironically, when this happened, it may have been an accident caused by foolish play. However, when we continually talk about something, we will eventually draw it to us —whether good or evil.

There have been several cases of actors meeting real-life tragedies that parallel a role they had once played in a film. These are not coincidences. When our words or thoughts (or role-playing) connect to the root of our soul (mind, will and emotions), they will come to pass. Words and thoughts are continually giving orders to the subconscious to carry out. For example, comedian Jim Carrey, who once lived in his car, decided to write himself a check for $10 million, projecting his future wealth. As the story goes, he carried this check around in his wallet as a reminder. Years later, he was reportedly paid $20 million for the movie, *The Cable Guy*.

We birth what we focus on, and what we focus on expands. If you want your quality of life to change, then beware of idle chatter and monitor your daily conversations at work, on the phone, and with family and friends. Most of us act and react to whatever is being said to us, as if we are on automatic pilot. Listen to your words. Stop and think: be slower to speak. All words pack a punch! Therefore, make a decision to clean up your thought life, which will have an effect on the words you speak. Your destiny depends on it!

THE WORDS YOU SPEAK TODAY, WILL BE THE LIFE YOU LIVE TOMORROW!

Notes

Spiritual Law

Every promise in the Word of God is a promise we can claim. Every word that Jesus ever spoke is a spiritual law that is set in cement. It is the truth for this world, regardless whether man chooses to believe it or not. What you believe does not change the truth. These laws rule and reign and govern your life, even when you are not aware of it. They can't be changed. They don't *sometimes* work—they *always* work! Once again: They ALWAYS work! God cannot—and will not—break His own spiritual laws for our individual situations. When we live our lives as if we are spitting in the wind, we take our chances where the spit might land.

If you have a financial need, but you are tight-fisted with your money for fear of not having enough, you will definitely not have enough. Whatever you are worried about will be drawn to you. If you focus your attention on what you do not have, you will continue to not have it. You get what you focus on, because that is what is taking root in your soul. So, instead of focusing on what you do not have, you must focus on what you want. If you speak lack, then you will have lack. If you speak provision, then you will have provision.

Thank God for your needs being met and then stop trying to figure out how you are going to make it happen. You have not, because you ask not. If you believe Jesus is the Son of God, then why is it so difficult to believe God's promises? You must believe them literally! Ask believing, not doubting in your heart (Mark 11:23-24). Lack of faith keeps God's promises from working. When we boldly proclaim God's Word, power is released. However, if we do not know God's Word, we lack overcoming power. We can't proclaim what we do not know.

The principles set forth in God's Word are meant for the good of mankind. When we are in obedience to these laws, God's hand of protection is upon us. Every area of our lives—whether it's financial, spiritual, relational, intellectual, or physical—is covered in the 66 books of the Bible. Every question we have ever had or ever will have is answered therein. The Bible is the instruction manual for a peaceful, well-balanced life —giving peace that passeth all understanding (Philippians 4:7-8).

Notice, that I didn't say a trouble-free life—I said we could have peace in the midst of our problems. No one escapes this life without hurdles to jump over. However, the direction we jump determines how long the challenges will last. The longer we murmur and complain about a situation, the longer the trial. When we decide to become content in our circumstances, as the Word of God tells us to do, the sooner we will have nothing to complain about and the sooner our prayers will be answered. If we become bitter in our trials, we will not become better.

God is no respecter of persons. He didn't specify that someone has to be a believer in order for their words to manifest. Many unscrupulous people have made their fortune by speaking and believing for a specific outcome. They have simply put spiritual law into motion without even knowing what makes it work—they just knew it works. Some put pictures on their refrigerator, while others speak daily affirmations until their desires come to pass. Our words, thoughts, actions, and what we focus on, WILL manifest!

This reminds me of my "miracle" van. Every time I spotted a van like the one I wanted, I would automatically say, "That's the one I want, there it is. Thank you God." Some months later a friend called and said, "There's a political meeting at a car dealership. Let's go." We went early, so just for fun we looked at some vehicles and there wasn't a van in sight. With time to spare, I decided to test drive a Ford Explorer. After that, we went into the restaurant on the lot. While we were eating, the salesman came in and asked me what I thought about the Explorer. I told him that I really wanted a van. While I was expressing my desire for a van, I stood up and passionately stated, "Look...you must know people. You're connected to other dealers, someone must have a van!" I thought I scared him, because he ran out of there without saying a word.

A few minutes later, he ran back in and told me that they had just taken in a van at an off-site lot where they detail their cars. He said, "If we leave right now we can get there before dark." So I jumped in his car and away we went.

As we approached the lot, I saw a white high-top van. I shouted, "That's the kind I want!" It was exactly what I had been thanking God for—A WHITE HIGH-TOP WITH A TV AND VCR! As we looked it over, I knew it was mine! There was only one obstacle—I had no money and no credit (actually I think that's two obstacles).However, since the van had my name written all over it, I went directly to the office of the owners and told them that they had a van that was meant for me. They lovingly sowed the down payment into my ministry, and by praying it through that night, all the credit fell in line. I told God "Thank You," and then nicely reminded Him that van payments would hinder me from being debt free. I then thanked Him ahead of time for paying off the loan.

Shortly thereafter, an assignment took me to Australia to assist a woman with her cancer treatments. Without a word from me about the van—she paid it off! Receiving that van was nothing more than spiritual law in motion. Below is a letter that Dr. Billye Brim's son, Terry, wrote concerning spiritual law after an amazing encounter with God.

God's Answer to Me[1]
By Terry Brim

This is a brief record of an experience with God that I had early Wednesday morning, August 18, 1999. It was Tuesday night, and I was concerned about the finances for the ministry and some other things that left me frustrated. In that frustration, I cried out to God, "Do any of Your promises or laws work?" I went to bed that night thinking, *I am going to figure out a way to generate the finances to finish the new administration building that we have started, and I might as well seek to find a wife without God's help, because I have somehow put myself in a position where I have missed the blessings of God.* I figured I was not praying enough or maybe not going to church enough—either it was something about me, or God's promises don't work for all.)

While in bed asleep, I was suddenly awakened and told to get a sheet of paper and a pen. I am going to tell you something—I knew it was God. I could sense His presence in the small trailer; otherwise, I

1Ref. Matthew 8:13, 9:29. Printed with permission from Terry Brim.

don't think I would have gotten up, because it was three o'clock in the morning. The following is what I wrote from the inspiration of God:

God does not bless or give to us according to what we deserve or what we may think is good, but according to the spiritual laws that He set into existence. Many of these laws, we became partakers in by just being born-again. (No effort on our part, it was paid for at Calvary.) There are other spiritual laws that it doesn't matter if a person is a born-again Christian or not, they will work. One that came to mind was, "Give and it shall be given unto you…" (Luke 6:38). Another was Mark 11:23, "That whosoever shall say unto this mountain, Be thou removed, and be thou cast into the sea; and shall not doubt in his heart, but shall believe that those things which he saith shall come to pass; he shall have whatsoever he saith."

These laws are powerful, so powerful and active, that they will keep a born-again Christian from receiving anything that God wants him to have. They will work in the positive, as well as the negative. For instance, go back to Mark 11:23. If we say the wrong or negative thing and believe it in our hearts, it will come to pass.

God also showed me Peter and reminded me of how he had denied Jesus three times prior to His death (Matthew 26:34, 69-75). When Jesus met with Peter after His resurrection, He asked Peter three times, "Peter do you love me?" (John 21:15-17). What Jesus was doing here was not only launching Peter's ministry, but He was stopping the effects of the words Peter had spoken when he denied Him. Jesus knew that Peter loved Him, and Peter knew that Jesus loved him. This was not the main issue. He was breaking the power over the words that were spoken! (Matthew 10:32-33.)

God also reminded me of Jesus' trial. Did you notice that Jesus never said a word in His defense? Yes, I noticed that.

"Want to know why?" God asked.

Yes, I do!

"If He had said one word in His defense, it would have started a spiritual law into action and stopped the plan of salvation!"

God brought me into remembrance of the verse that states that a double-minded man will receive nothing (James 1:6-8). It is because he will say one thing, which puts a law into action, and then turn around and say the complete opposite, which causes the laws he spoke to cancel each other out! He showed me that in church, people will say the right things. In prayer, they will say the right things. However, out in the battles of life, they will say the wrong things—sometimes even just outside the church door.

I asked God, "If these laws are a constant and if they work for even the non-believer as well as for the weakest Christian, why do we need to read the Bible, go to church, or listen to tapes?"

God answered me by showing me one of His natural laws. He asked me, "What happens when an acid and a base react?"

I answered and said, "You get a salt and a water." (I had taken chemistry in school.)

God said, "It works every time because it is My law." Then He showed me that if the acid and the base are strong, they will produce these products (salt and water) quickly and vigorously. "Let My law represent the acid, a strong acid, and let your faith represent the base. If you have a weak base (or faith), the law will still work, but it will be slow. You need to increase the strength of your base if you want a strong reaction. The same goes for your faith, and you increase your faith by hearing the Word of God."

When you are first born again, you do not receive the full measure of faith because you would be like a child with a loaded gun. God is fair and just. He cannot stop the effects of the laws just because of our situation. God told me that He created the universe with the same laws, and He created man in His likeness and expected man to use these laws just like Him. "By this law, I created the universe. I did not withhold this law from man (Mark 11:23-24). Satan knew the power of this law. It is the weapon he used to try to defeat me (Isaiah 14). But...against God it cannot..."

So I said, "God, what do I need to do?"

God told me to open my spiritual eyes. He said, "You need to know that you are in covenant with

Me; everything that is Mine is yours, and everything that is yours is Mine."

I do this now by taking communion first thing in the morning. God also has me read Matthew chapter 27 concerning the crucifixion of Jesus, so that I will know the price that was paid so that I may belong to and work with God. It also establishes the fact that He cares for me and my girls, and no matter what the devil may do or situations that arise, I know I can conquer it; for I am in covenant with God.

Another way to remember all God taught me is to just look at what God has already created: trees, water, wildlife, stars, the sun, the moon, and most importantly, you and me. I know that God can and will provide and see to it that His laws do not fail. In closing, this is what God told me, "Don't be discouraged. I have not abandoned you, no matter what you have done." Remember, He does not bless us by what we deserve, but by what we put into practice.

The Spirit Realm

We are not human beings going through temporary spiritual experiences—we are spiritual beings going through temporary human experiences. Our body is only a temporary house for the Holy Spirit to dwell in. Our "humanness" holds us back from experiencing a higher dimension of living. Living on this planet, we only see and hear what is in our everyday sphere—without a care or a thought of what is happening in the spirit realm all around us. In this unseen realm, God's angels and Satan's demons are doing battle in the heavenlies. The *Star Wars* concept of good and evil is very real. *This Present Darkness,* written by Frank Peretti, paints an excellent picture of how the spirit realm operates.

If our physical eyes could see what is taking place in the unseen spirit world, we would have instant faith. The Bible tells us that Satan and his demons will wreak havoc in the world until Jesus returns. This is the reason why most everything is in chaos. The daily news clearly reveals the increasing turmoil in our world. Joining peace movements, as commendable as that is, will never bring peace. This is one example of positive thinking that cannot manifest, because it is against the Word of God. The Bible clearly states that there will always be wars and rumors of wars (Matthew 24:6).

Whatever is written is law! When the Bible tells us what is going to take place and we are out there trying to make something else happen, we are simply spinning our wheels. If we all loved our fellow man the way God instructed us to, we would have peace. However, if we cannot even get along with our family and friends, how do we think that we can have peace on a planet with millions of people —all with their own agenda issues?

For we wrestle not against flesh and blood, but against principalities, against powers, against the rulers of the

darkness of this world, against spiritual wickedness in
high places.

Ephesians 6:12

Some years ago, while visiting my mother in the
mountains of Pennsylvania, I had a strange encounter
(vision). As I laid my head down on the sofa, I looked out
of the picture window that was facing me. A bright light
on the top of the mountain caught my eye. It was unusual,
because at night these mountains are pitch-dark for miles
around, unless the moon is shining. Bewildered, I got up
and stared out the window. Suddenly the light started
moving down the mountain and appeared as a floating
angel. When it was about eye level to me, the angel-like
figure headed straight toward me, but it soon turned into
something that looked like a torpedo with dragon scales.
This odd-looking creature looked like it was going to
come straight through the window.

As I continued to stare, I backed up and sat down on
the sofa. Without forethought, I found myself repeating,
"Jesus, Jesus, Jesus, Jesus, Jesus…" over and over as fast as
I could. Then, just as suddenly as it had appeared, this
"thing" reversed its direction, went back up the mountain,
and the light went out. When I phoned my sister, Jo-Anna,
to tell her what I had experienced, she said, "You just had
a visit from Satan."

*...for Satan himself is transformed into an angel of
light.*

II Corinthians 11: 14

Just because you may not see the demons lurking about,
does not mean that they are not there. Time is short! Satan is
working overtime to do as much damage as he can. His
demons are flitting about, obeying assignments to kill, steal
and destroy. However, there is nothing to fear if you, "Submit
yourselves therefore to God. Resist the devil and he will flee
from you" (James 4:7).

The name of Jesus has power all by itself.

If you are ever in harm's way—call on the name of Jesus!

Fear activates the devil—faith brings God on the scene.

Until we seek the truth and apply it, life will continue to
be a battle of unrest. Casting our cares on the Lord puts the
battle in His hands. Speaking God's promises found in His
Word activates the heavens to bring the promise to pass on
waves of glory.

Electromagnetic Waves

The atmosphere is electrically charged. Electrical frequencies actually carry our spoken words and thoughts to
their destination —the Kingdom of God or the physical universe. Television, radio, computers, and all of the remarkable technology that we have today, operate on these electro-

magnetic waves, sending their information on different frequencies in a particular direction. Everything has an electrical charge, including you and me (inside of every protein
are sound frequencies). Therefore, our bodies are receivers
that send forth energy—similar to a battery. Our hands can
be likened to jumper cables (healing hands). The human
battery is charged during a good night's sleep, being regen-
erated by the One who electrifies the entire universe—God
himself. Scientists recognize this energy; however, they
don't always acknowledge the "source."

Although I never quite understood this energy business,
one day I finally "got it"—literally! At one of my ladies
prayer meetings one afternoon in Burbank, California, my
arms and hands became fully charged with electricity. My
arms became rigid and would not bend. It was as if electricity was coming out of my finger tips, and all I could do was
point my arms straight in front of me. As I pointed to each
woman, the Holy Spirit led me to say, "Whatever you want,
you can have—just say it!" When we were done praying,
the electrical current subsided.

During this prayer meeting, a pastor's wife told us that
the IRS had informed her and her husband that they owed a
large sum of money, which they did not have. The women
gathered around her and prayed for God to intervene and
give her favor in this situation. A short time later, the pastor
and his wife received another letter from the IRS canceling

their debt. The best part of this story is that the IRS also informed the pastor that they (the IRS) actually owed them money, and sent them a substantial check. Favor like this excites me! Answered prayer excites me! Think about it... we have access to the very power that holds the entire universe in place! We have a direct hotline to our heavenly Father—we just need to plug in!

SAY WHAT YOU WANT—UNTIL YOU BELIEVE YOU CAN HAVE IT!

Wired
from
Childhood

We have all been programmed by words from our childhood. Parents, teachers, relatives, friends, and the media
have formed our thinking, which in turn has formed our
speech. As adults, we believe what we believe about the
world around us from reading the newspaper and listening
to the news. We can either accept or reject what our ears
and eyes take in, but we usually receive information and
opinions at face value. Unfortunately, when we hear something often enough and it comes from a source that we trust,
it becomes truth to us (whether or not it is). Politicians also
know this and use it to their advantage.

Our daily lives are constantly being bombarded with the
words of other people. Consequently, our computer-like

brains become wired with positive or negative current—so to speak. It is common to hear people say, "Think positive." Yet most folks do not have a true understanding of the power behind positive or negative words. I'm not talking about your everyday generalization about "thinking positive," but rather the effects of positive and negative thoughts and words. The Bible tells us, "As a man thinketh so is he!" (Proverbs 23:7). Likewise, as a man speaketh so is he- as a man believeth so is he!

A THOUGHT turns into an ACTION

Which develops a HABIT

That becomes part of our CHARACTER

That determines our DESTINY

My Happy Home

I was so fortunate to be have been raised by my loving grandparents,who never put me down. They always encouraged my heart's desires and talents. Our loving home was based on love, peace, and joy. It was also filled with kind and loving words. Music usually filled the air from my Grandpap's radio every morning, as my Gramy cooked my breakfast before school. Other times, Gramy would play hymns on the piano, many of which she wrote.

Gramy was the wisest person I have ever known. She never raised her voice or her hand to me. Gramy and Grandpap respected me, even when I did not deserve it. In my teens, I started hanging around with, what Gramy thought were some undesirable classmates, which caused her great concern. One particular day, Gramy told me to come home directly after band practice, instead of hanging out with my new friends. However, I didn't listen and decided to go for a joy-ride with a carload of my new buddies.

As we were driving up a very narrow mountain road, the guy who was driving and his girlfriend began to fight. He started to speed, speeding and weaving all over the road. Suddenly, one of the tires blew and the car ran into the mountain. His girlfriend was thrown out of the car and lost a few teeth. The rest of us were just shaken up a bit. If the car had veered to the other side of the road, we would have gone over a huge cliff. God had mercy on us!

After I was checked out at the hospital, a policeman took me home, where Gramy was waiting on the porch. She wasn't exactly happy, but she never threw the fact that I had been disobedient in my face. She knew that going to my room and thinking about what I had done would be punishment enough. If she had berated me with "I told you so," or other words of condemnation, I would probably have rebelled even more.

Gramy could see the "brat" in me emerging and knew she needed to "nip it in the bud." One day she sat me down and showed me a brochure of a girls school in Philadelphia.

She calmly painted a very dismal picture of what it would be like to live there. In her loving way, Gramy gave me the choice to either follow the rules at home or go to the girls school. My heart and mind immediately snapped to attention. I was not about to lose my happy home!

Children Learn What They Live

Many children are being emotionally "stunted" by negative words. Words can cripple the very people you love the most. Words bring victory or defeat in any given situation. *Our words either heal or hurt—bless or curse!* We are all who we are today because of WORDS! Please get this! Words do not just affect children temporarily. Negative, degrading words leave permanent scars and produce rebellious and troubled children, as well as adults. On the other hand, positive, uplifting words produce confident and productive children and adults.

Children are walking antennas and are much more aware than adults give them credit for being. When mothers and fathers argue in front of their children,this adversely affects their impressionable minds. They may look like they are not paying attention, but they are really taking it all in. If you are a single parent, I implore you not to talk bad about your ex! This puts children in the middle, thinking that they need to take sides. It causes confusion because they love both parents. Regardless of your feelings, Do Not turn a child against their mother or father, or anyone—there is a price to pay if you do! The presence of anger, foul words, and immoral practices around children of any age is like planting poison seeds in them. Each new upset waters the poison seed until it is fully grown—when your actions become their actions!

Children's sponge-like brains are continually soaking up what they see and hear. All that information, whether positive or negative, is forever etched in their minds—molding and shaping them into the person that they eventually become. Every bit of this will surface at some point in their life, affecting their relationships, either in a positive or negative way. For instance, a mother may ask, "Where did my Jimmy learn to lie?" From you, of course—Mom and Dad—when you told Jimmy to tell the person on the phone that you were not at home when you really were. That sounds so harmless, doesn't it? It was just a little "white lie."When Jimmy gets older, his employer may ask him, "Why don't you keep your word and do what you say you're going to?"Jimmy will have all kinds of excuses,because he doesn't believe that he did anything wrong. In fact, he thinks that his boss is making a big deal over nothing. However, the reality is that Jimmy doesn't keep his word because his mom and dad taught him that a person's word is unimportant, every time they broke a childhood promise to him.

If a child lives with criticism,

He learns to condemn.

If a child lives with hostility,

He learns to fight.

If a child lives with ridicule,

He learns to be shy.

If a child lives with shame,

He learns to feel guilty.

If a child lives with tolerance,

He learns to be patient.

If a child lives with encouragement,

He learns confidence.

If a child lives with praise,

He learns to appreciate.

If a child lives with fairness,

He learns justice.

If a child lives with security,

He learns to have faith.

If a child lives with approval,

He learns to like himself.

If a child lives with acceptance & friendship,

He learns to find love in the world.

Dorothy Law Nolte

Listen and Encourage

When children share an idea or a desire to do something and their parents ignore them, their spirit is immediately crushed. By ignoring their children, parents are conveying that their thoughts and desires are not important. Consequently, the children are "devalued" and feel unimportant. After a few experiences like this, children will "shut down" and quit sharing things with their parents. Once a small child looked me in the eye and asked, "Why don't grown-ups ever listen to kids?" Clearly, this heartbroken child felt invisible and never felt validated as a person.

Children who believe that they are an "inconvenience" or feel unloved, grow up thinking that they have no worth. Their decisions tend to sabotage their life, keeping them in a state of despair and unhappiness—many times resulting in life-long depression. Listen to your children! Build them up! Praise them! Speak to them, as if they already were the person you want them to be, and that is what they will become.

A merry heart maketh a cheerful countenance; but by sorrow of the heart the spirit is broken.

Proverbs 15:13

When we think back to our childhood, what words do we remember? If a classmate called us "banana nose," or a parent said we were "stupid," we never forget it. We recall all the negative things said to us—forever! It's common for a parent to blurt out remarks such as, "You're driving me crazy! Can't you do anything right? I wish you were never born!" These hurtful words eventually turn into anger and resentment toward the parent(s).

Negative words strip children of their confidence and self-worth, wiring them with negative circuitry for a lifetime. Parents are famous for yelling, "How many times do I have to tell you?" The only thing that these shouting matches do is raise one's blood pressure. The more that children hear yelling and put-downs, the more they will rebel. In essence, their parents are teaching them how to communicate in a negative manner. The odds for these children to have healthy, well-balanced relationships in the future are nil. However, when loving, godly principles are applied to renew their minds, the pain from the past will be erased as if it never happened.

Speaking harshly to people does not work! However, kind, loving talk coupled with the right action does! Anger settles in the soul long before it surfaces. When rebellion starts, parents think it came out of nowhere, when in fact it has been brewing for a long time. Parents are usually clueless as to why their children went down the wrong path. They become confused and wonder what they did wrong—believing that they raised their children the best way they knew how. However, the truth is that the parents did exactly what they knew to do—repeating what their parents had said and done to them. It is a vicious cycle and until it is broken, it will continue throughout generations.

Old patterns are difficult to break until the chains of bondage have been severed. Even when a child says, "I'll never be like my dad," he inevitably ends up being "just like his dad." Of course, there are some instances in which a person makes a conscious decision to escape his circumstances in order to ensure that his life is different from what he was raised in. A good example of this can be found in a profound, true story in Dave Pelzer's book, *A Child Called It*.

Positive Discipline

Children who act up are crying for attention. They receive their much-needed attention by not conforming, even in adulthood. The lack of loving attention also produces resentment and anger. Speaking words of love over your children will bring God's light into your home and fill your children with confidence. *"I love you! Jesus loves you! You are a child of God! You have great potential! God has a special purpose for you to fulfill that no one else can do! I'm proud to be your mother/ father!"* Praising your children and encouraging their gifts and talents will take them to a higher plain. When you pick at their flaws, their flaws grow bigger.

Refrain from using the words "don't" or "you should." By doing this, you will be way ahead in the parenting game.

Most children automatically do the opposite of what they are told. That is what a child does, regardless of age. For small children, refrain from saying things like, "Didn't I tell you to pick up your toys?" The alternative is, "Did you pick up your toys so we can have dinner, or read a story, or take a walk?" If your tone is pleasant and your words are positive, you will not have any correctional issues.

Once when my nephew, Aron, was a young boy, he received a handful of candy in Sunday school. When his mother, sister and I came out of church, his mother told him to share the candy with his sister, but he refused. Regardless of how we pleaded, he wasn't about to part with his "precious" candy. So, I nicely asked him, "Do you enjoy being selfish ... does it make you feel good?" He thought about this for a few seconds, and all of a sudden he was giving us all candy —and he actually enjoyed doing it. *When we need to confront someone, regardless of age, asking questions puts the ball in their court, creating a less defensive atmosphere.*

Another reverse psychology moment with Aron occurred when he came to stay with me once during vacation. He was looking forward to a birthday party that he was invited to attend. However, when it was time for him to get ready to go to the party, he got dressed without taking his bath.

So, I (Auntie) said, "You didn't take your bath yet."

Aron: "I'm not going to take a bath."

Auntie: "You want to be clean to go to the party don't you?"

Aron: "No, I'm not taking a bath."

So I sweetly said, "That's okay; you don't have to go to the party."

Aron quickly ran into the bathroom, took off his clothes, and jumped into the bathtub. He was happy, I was happy, and he went to the party. He made his own choice without anyone getting upset.

Children like choices. The earlier you start with positive discipline, the easier it will be. However, it's never too late. Keep in mind that whatever you say to your child, you must back up. Your word is only as good as the action behind it. How many times do we hear parents say, "If you do that one more time, I'm going to punish you?" Yet, the parent continues to have a screaming match, instead of following through with the punishment. Soon the child is in charge of the household. When this happens, the child will "reel out of control."Children are simply begging for discipline! Where there is no discipline, children feel unstable. Children with fair boundaries grow up feeling secure.

Don't Sweat the Small Stuff

It is common for some parents to push their will on their children, which in turn stifles their child's creativity and individualism. Parents may unconsciously want to live their failed dreams through their children. Therefore, they decide what music or sports activities their children will participate in, instead of allowing their children to pursue their own interests. If you are doing that —STOP! God puts interests in each of us, young and old, for a reason and He will use them for His purposes. If a young person shows talent and passion for something and they are denied the development of it, then they are receiving a "what's the use" message. This will affect what they do for their entire lives. They will feel that regardless of what they do, it will not pay off. They would rather sabotage their own life than risk failure or another disappointment.

Parents—encourage your child's desires, even if they do not stick with it. Do not force them to stick with it if they decide they are no longer interested. We all change our minds. Let them discover their niche by being adventurous and exploring all options. Children who have been given freedom to develop their individualism are the ones who go out and do great things in life. However, it is never too late for them to fulfill their dreams. It only takes an encouraging word from the right person at the right time!

The best advice that I can give to parents is "don't sweat the small stuff." When parents try to raise perfect children, it backfires on them. For instance, when children are being told how to act at every turn—Sit up straight...don't lean on the table...don't run, you might hurt yourself...go out and play, but don't get dirty...use your fork, not your spoon... smile, don't smile—you are setting them up to be angry adults. Save your breath! Children do not learn what they are being told; they learn by example.

Telling never teaches children anything! Instead, they learn and repeat what they see their parents doing, and they always remember and learn what they are lovingly shown. When a child is continually berated, it's like chopping away at their self-worth, bit by bit. Soon, that young child will start to believe that whatever he does will never be good enough. He becomes frustrated and resentful. There is nothing that children want more than for their parents to be proud of them.

When teaching, remember:

> You hear, you forget.
> You see, you remember.
> You do, you understand.

Parents naturally think that they are teaching their children what is best for them. However, the message the children receive from constant critical-instruction is that they can't please their parents. They don't know how to make you proud of them, so they eventually quit trying. They lose their joy—and this is easily seen in their eyes. Soon, you will see signs of emotional trouble: wetting the bed, stealing, lying, hiding things, withdrawing, breaking toys, and other things like this. Children and adults need more praise and less criticism! Children need about 32 uplifting words of encouragement to negate one negative comment.

Allow these little ones to be children. Let me make it clear—there is a big difference between control and discipline! If the children are not breaking God's commandments or being unruly, then there is no need to constantly be on their case. Let them develop their own special personalities. Guide and direct them through God's Word, praying with them daily. Look them in the eyes and tell them that you love them—showering them with lots of hugs and kisses.

Understand that no child has ever been perfectly parented. Trying to get a parent to act differently, or still trying as an adult to get our childhood expectations fulfilled, will only lead to disappointment. If everyone hid behind their story, no one would act properly. Everyone has a story—and every story determines how we look at life and what we think of ourselves. We will either be a positive or negative personality, emotionally healthy or a victim, a self-centered bellyacher or one who reaches out to uplift others.

The battles of life are never won until the mind is renewed! This includes everyone! Past hurts and unpleasant memories, the world's brainwashing, and the demons from hell that keep "stinkin thinkin" rolling around in your head must be deleted! The past is the past -leave it there! If you dwell on the past, you're stifling your future. To start the renewing process, a person must be teachable and welcome correction. The renewing of the mind starts by humbling ourselves before the Lord. By focusing on Jesus and His all powerful living words, your heart will be healed and your mind renewed.

Repeat the following confessions often from Charles Capps' book[2]—post them as reminders:

> "I receive the spirit of wisdom and revelation in the knowledge of Him. The eyes of my understanding being enlightened, I am not conformed to this world, but am transformed by the renewing of my mind. My mind is renewed by the Word of God."
>
> Ephesians 1:17-18; Romans 12:2

> "The peace of God which passeth all understanding keeps my heart and my mind through Christ Jesus. And all things which are good, and pure, and perfect, and lovely and of good report, I think on these things."
>
> Philippians 4:7-8

START EVERYDAY WITH
A CLEAN SLATE —
GOD'S MERCIES ARE NEW EVERY MORNING.

---

2 Charles Capps, *The Tongue: A Creative Force.* (England, Arkansas: Capps Publishing, 1976). Reprinted by permission of the publisher.

Notes

Forgive
&
Get Over It

Those who whine about their past or their present
develop a victim mentality and harbor grudges and unforgiveness. One of the most important things that I have
realized is that forgiveness is necessary in order to be an
overcomer in life. It doesn't matter what anyone has said to
you, about you, or how they have treated you; you MUST
forgive. God has forgiven us and if we do not forgive others,
God will not forgive us (Matthew 6:14,15; Luke 6:37).

Unforgiveness and bitterness can foster disease in the
body, as well as hinder our prayers and our relationship with
our heavenly Father. Unresolved strife and unforgiveness
can also damage our earthly relationships. Don't wait for the
other person to shape up and do the right thing so you can

show them love and forgiveness, because it does not work that way. The instruction manual for life—the Bible—clearly tells us that LOVE is the bottom line. Love your enemies and you will see miracles.

There are two things that will help with self-righteous indignation. First, look at the person through the eyes of Jesus. In His eyes, we are all equal and He loves us all the same. Second, stop taking things personally. Removing one's self from any given situation is totally freeing. Do not be drawn into other people's "stuff." Yes, it is easier said than done, but until one learns to do this, the upsets will continue.

It Isn't What Happens to Us That Ruins Us — It's Our Response to What Happens.

The next time you start to lose it, take a deep breath, turn around in a circle three times, and shout "Jesus!" The only reason we get upset is because of past issues that have instilled fears, insecurities, or out-of-control egos. Former New York mayor, Rudolph Giuliani was noticeably calm during the 9/11 aftermath at Ground Zero. He later attributed this to his father, who told him, "The more chaos around you, the calmer you must be."

When you let your emotions control you, then the one who makes you angry is the one who is in control. If you act and react in love, it will drive them crazy! Gramy always said, "Kill them with kindness." Regardless of how despicable the other person is or how heinous the crime they may have committed, Jesus says we must forgive them. If someone is continually doing you wrong, you may ask yourself, "How many times do I have to forgive them?" When Peter asked the Lord in Matthew 18: 21, how often he had to forgive his brother, Jesus told him 70 times 7.

Most definitely, we must forgive. However, that does not mean that we are to be doormats either. You have no right to complain about what you are allowing. In case this hits home, make a sign and hang it up as a constant reminder. You may say, "But, there is no way out!" Yes, there is, dear friend—you just don't want to take it. Fear of the unknown keeps you stuck. THE ONLY WAY OUT IS UP! With God's help, face the fear head-on and it will go away. If you are relying on yourself to fix the problem without God's help, there may be no way out—in fact, it may even get worse. These challenges help grow us up and strengthen us.

If you are operating from a bitter, angry heart, then your mind, will, and emotions need softened and humbled. Allow God to do spiritual surgery on your heart. Repentance is the first step—ask God for forgiveness and then forgive everyone you have anything against. Everyone! We can say that we forgive, but until we no longer have that scenario playing over and over in our heads about what someone did to us and how we are going to get even, we have not forgiven. If we continually talk about it, we have not forgiven. If we have a need to tell others about it, we have not forgiven. Love covers a multitude of sins. When we decide to love the person who wronged us, God will take care of it—in His time, in His way. There is no need to defend ourselves when we allow God to come on the scene. God sees it all!

Vengeance is mine; I will repay, saith the Lord.

Romans 12:19

Once in awhile, you will hear of a situation on the news in which a mother has gone to a prison and forgiven the person who murdered her child. Most people cannot understand how anyone could forgive something like this that seems so"unforgivable." According to the world and our natural thinking, this is impossible. However, when the love of God reigns in your heart, you connect with the supernatural.

With men this is impossible, but with God all things are possible.

Matthew 19:26

Unforgiveness is like drinking poison and expecting the other person to die. Unforgiveness takes root and grows like a cancer. Whatever eats away at our emotions, will eventually eat away at our bodies. When you forgive someone, it does not mean that you condone what they have done. It simply means that you have decided to love them and leave the judging to God. Remember, if you lash out at others about their imperfections and shortcomings, at some point you will be on the other end of the lashing. It is easy to love and forgive those who love us, but we are called to love and forgive the "unlovable." We will all be treated the way we treat others!

Whatsoever a man soweth, that shall he also reap.

Galatians 6:7

The people who act the worst, are usually the ones who need love the most. Rejecting them or treating them unkindly fuels their fire of self-destruction. We haven't walked in their shoes. God is watching how we act and react to the unlovely. Today, our world is filled with violence, cruelty and hatred like I have not known in my lifetime. Godless, unforgiving hearts want someone to pay for every little thing. There is no such thing as a "simple accident" anymore—someone must pay the price, even for the slip of the tongue. People are not free to have an opinion unless it fits the "politically correct" mold. Love is the missing ingredient!

If you are the one who is always being offended, STOP IT! As I have said, do not take things personally. If it is not your problem or a matter of life and death, leave it alone! If the problem is close to home and cannot be avoided, then "love"the problem away. The only antidote to all of our woes is love and forgiveness. Love is a decision—decide to love! A heart that loves, automatically forgives.

UNFORGIVENESS IS THE SAME THING
AS DRINKING POISON AND EXPECTING THE
OTHER PERSON TO DIE.

Perfect Love

Perfect love casteth out fear.
He that feareth is not made perfect in love.

I John 4:18

Everyone needs to be loved. The emotion of love is a powerful tool. Love heals, inspires, rejuvenates, creates a safety zone, and brings us closer to God. Love is a basic ingredient for health. If there is no love in our life, we cannot sustain a healthy heart. True love is selfless and free from fear, pouring itself out upon the object of its affection without demanding anything in return. Love sees no wrong and ceases to be jealous or vengeful.

However, much of the time our love is conditional and selfish. We expect others to act and react in a way that suits us. Relationships can only be whole, happy and fulfilling when we love God's way. Give perfect love and you will receive perfect love. You will never receive what you have never given. The balance of God's law literally hangs on this one thing that He commands us to do —love. Where love dwells, everything else will be a piece of cake.

Love Is the Answer

Love one another, as I have loved you.

John 15:12

Marriages suffer because of constant criticism between spouses. Many times couples treat each other as though they are enemies, forgetting that they are on the same side. There is an old saying: "No man is your enemy, no man is your friend, every man is your teacher." Each person who comes into our lives is there for a definite purpose; each to learn something from the other. The first step to loving is to stop being critical of others and realize that everyone has value and something to contribute. Love will free us from destructive emotions. You will know you are free when nothing pushes your buttons!

We usually love when we are loved in return; however, pure love is unconditional. If we all decided to love our fellow man the way God intended, we would have world peace in 24 hours. According to God's Word, however, we know that world peace will only happen when Jesus returns., So… if we want to have peace in our individual lives, here and now, LOVE IS THE ANSWER!

God Is Love

That Christ may dwell in your hearts by faith;
that ye, being rooted and grounded in love...

Ephesians 3: 17

There was a woman I knew who put down her husband every time she opened her mouth. He could never do anything right in her eyes. This built up resentment in him. Consequently, he lost the desire to be romantic towards her. She did not respect him and respect is what men need the most.

One day after she became aware of her negative attitude, she made a conscious decision to start building up her husband, instead of tearing him down. She started greeting him after work with a smile and complimented him every chance she got. Soon his posture improved, as well as his affection towards her.

Take a good long look at the person you once adored, before you became familiar with their "ugly stuff." Forget about your needs for a moment, and concentrate on making the "love of your life" happy. The trick to this is to change your language! Changing your language will automatically change your actions.

Women, remember, men thrive on respect —so let him be "king of the castle." Men, if you want your wife to treat you like a king, then cherish her and treat her like your queen. Love and cherish each other using words of love— life is too short! Think of your spouse as your best friend. Speak positive words over them. Be diligent! It takes 21 days to form a habit, so stick with it. Eventually you won't even remember what you were fussing about. DO NOT GIVE UP! Follow the path of love, for God is Love.

Love Never Fails

...Thou shalt love thy neighbor as thyself.

Romans 13:9

When there are difficulties with individuals, whether in the work place or with family and friends, instead of speaking against that person, start speaking blessings over them. Celebrate who they are in the eyes of Jesus. Soon that difficult person will no longer be an issue. For example, once God put it on my heart to pray for a certain politician who I really wasn't very fond of. After praying for him a few times, I had a newfound compassion for him. God revealed to me that he was a man racked with pain. Some time later, he developed brain cancer and died.

Most diseases and unhappiness come from violating the "law of love." Man's criticism, hate and resentment that he spews, returns as sickness and sorrow. But the man who gains knowledge of spiritual law and applies it to his life finds perfect love. Notice that I did not say he finds a perfect marriage or perfect relationships; I said "perfect love."

LOVE IS NOT:

- Abusive
- Belittling
- Controlling
- Critical
- Demeaning
- Shaming
- Manipulative
- Negative

First Corinthians Chapter 13 (known as the Love Chapter) tells us:

Love suffers long, and is kind; love does not envy; love does not parade itself, is not puffed up; does not behave rudely, does not seek its own, is not provoked, thinks no evil; does not rejoice in iniquity, but rejoices in the truth; bears all things, believes all things, hopes all things, endures all things. Love never fails.

(Vv. 4-8 NKJV)

The Heart and Mind Connection

Keep thy heart with all diligence, for out of it are the issues of life.

Proverbs 4:23

Every 23 seconds, the heart pumps the blood through the body, reaching every cell.

Life is in the blood—God is the giver of life.

When we need a change in our life, it often means that we need a change of heart. We need to allow God to do emotional heart surgery. First, you must make the decision to change. This gives God permission to intervene in the healing of your heart and the renewing of your mind. Our hearts are individual and personal to God. There is a void in everyone's heart that only the Creator can fill! The Bible says that He knows our hearts.

The World Looks On the Outward Appearance, but the Lord Looks On the Heart

There are definite mind and heart connections. Research has shown that when a heart is implanted into another person, the recipient will take on the traits of the donor. This reminds me of a story of a woman who received the heart of a young man. This woman was not a drinker, but after receiving her new heart, she heard herself say, "I want a beer." Personality traits and cravings change for many who have experienced living with someone else's heart. This happens because the heart is a storehouse of life's experiences and emotions, making us who we have become since birth. Obviously, the heart is much more than just a muscle.

Our thoughts have a tremendous influence on the health of our heart. Living in a harmonious environment and having happy thoughts and positive emotions can prevent coronary artery disease. The heart and mind are connected through the autonomic nervous system, which can affect the heart rate and blood pressure. Having negative emotions such as fear, anger, jealousy, or being a workaholic, or highly demanding individual releases adrenaline and increases a person's vulnerability to a heart attack.

Every thought influences the heart. When we hurt (I mean really hurt), we sometimes clutch our chest, because the pain is so "unbearable." People literally die of broken hearts.

Even though the heart is a symbol of love, it can be filled with anger, bitterness, resentment, and unforgiveness. These "emotional poisons" must be eliminated in order to obtain health and happiness. We must learn to let "it" go— whatever "it" is. LET "IT" GO!

You are poisoned by bitterness and bound by iniquity.

Acts 8:23

Those who have experienced emotional abuse have had their heart and soul mutilated. Rejection, shame, and guilt, send them through life feeling "unworthy." These deep wounds hinder them from living free and enjoying healthy, happy relationships. All abuse is traumatic; however, emotional abuse damages the heart and leads individuals to emotionally abuse themselves on a daily basis. Emotional abuse is at the root of all other types of abuse. The most damaging aspect of physical, sexual, and mental abuse is the devastation to our hearts and souls from being betrayed by those we love and trust.

"Love Me When I Least Deserve It, Because That's When I Really Need It."
(Swedish Proverb)

Dr. Paul Hegstrom from Life Skills International in Colorado, says that the following abuses suffered before the age of nine, can cause arrested development—a condition in which development has stopped prematurely:

1. Rejection

2. Incest

3. Molestation

4. Emotional Abuse

5. Physical Abuse

These abuses will create an internal perception of powerlessness for our entire lives unless they are dealt with. Bruises to the body fade away; however, bruises to the heart and soul remain—until we start focusing on God's healing touch. Emotional abuse sometimes makes it harder to get in touch with our real issues because such abuse isn't always obvious: It could be the subtle way in which we were looked at, how someone said our name, or perhaps it was not being seen or heard.

We are emotional beings and we cannot be whole and healthy, without having an emotionally honest relationship with ourselves. When we get in touch with our emotions and take a look at our issues, that is the beginning of healing for our broken hearts and wounded souls. It is not always easy to pinpoint the root of the emotion, due to unhealed "childhood wounds." When we get upset, we might often be reacting as that insecure, scared little child of years ago. Why else would we get so angry? We have all seen people act and react crazy over the least little things. When we are emotionally healthy and free, our buttons do not get pushed!

Emotions are experienced in the heart and mind and affect us positively or negatively. I could write an entire book on this subject. However, this brief synopsis is for those who need to start dealing with their past emotional issues. Yes, it is life changing to understand the power of the spoken word, and be able to speak forth our hearts' desires; however, God wants us whole and healthy in every area of our lives.

Ask God to reveal those areas in your life that need healing and deliverance. Many people deny that they have anything to deal with. However, most everyone has been haunted by their childhood or adulthood traumas in some way or another. If you are not happy, have bouts of anger, or if chaos surrounds you, start facing your deep-rooted emotions so you can start living a fulfilled life.

1. Love is the answer!

2. Love unconditionally.

3. Refrain from being critical towards anyone—speak blessings over them. Send them love.

4. Deal with "emotional poisons"—asking God to reveal the areas in your life that need healed and delivered.

LET NOT YOUR HEART BE TROUBLED!

CHAPTER SIX

If You Can't Say Anything Good— Shut Up

When I moved to California in my early twenties, my best friend said to me, "You never say anything bad about anyone." I was surprised to hear that, because I had never really thought about that. To my recollection, when I was younger, we never talked negatively about people in our home. Since I grew up in a small town of "good folks," I naively assumed the world and everybody in it, was "good."However, when I joined the "fast paced" world and "big city" living, I found out differently.

In the late 80's and early 90's, I attended several prayer meetings in the Hollywood area. Some consisted of more gossip than prayer. Prayer gossip goes like this: "I'm just telling you this about Jane so you will know how to pray."

When I first heard people do this, I thought we needed to know all the dirt before we could ask God to clean it up. Oh, how we can be so misled! God knows the person and the need. Prayers should not include the ugly details.

> *Let no corrupt communication proceed out of your*
> *mouth, but that which is good to the use of edifying,*
> *that it may minister grace unto the hearers.*
>
> Ephesians 4:29

Listening to cable news is very difficult these days because the newscasters are usually chewing people up and spitting them out. Character assassination sells. If you find yourself saying that you hate someone, you better retract those words immediately. Hate is a strong word! How can you hate someone whose heart you do not know? We degrade others to make our insecure selves look better. God calls us to cover others' sin—never tell others about it. Pray for them! Change starts with each of us. Look at others through the eyes of Jesus and lift them up, instead of tearing them down. Reaching out with loving words can cause people to bloom like a bright colored flower.

Kick the Negative Habit

If you think and speak negatively, you are sabotaging your life and most likely the lives of those around you. Test yourself! Do you automatically respond with a negative comment when someone shares something with you? Do you poke fun at other people's dreams? When you encourage the goals and dreams of others and help them become successful, you will become successful. Listen to what your mouth is saying.

What Comes Out of Your Mouth, Reveals the Condition of Your Heart!

Put a tape recorder on and let it play for a few hours while you are talking with others. Better yet, tell someone to record you when you are unaware. When you hear yourself speak, you will know what needs corrected. The words you use will vary depending on who you are talking to. If you are putting on a "kissy face," and your words are dripping like honey to friends and associates, but you are a holy terror at home, there is a chink in the armor. Put yourself on a word watch! Listen to what you are saying. If your speech is phony because you are trying to keep up appearances, get to the bottom of your insecurities. Do some soul-searching. If you have an anger problem, you most likely have a forgiveness problem (read the forgiveness chapter again and again). Forgiveness is the first step to healing.

Tips for a Happy Tongue:

1. When gossip starts around you, change the subject or depart. Those who will gossip to you, will gossip about you.

2. When anger rises up and you know you are about to say something you shouldn't, remember this foolproof tip: Take a deep breath, turn around in a circle three times and shout, "JE-SUS."

3. Keep a smile on your face and one in your heart.

The words of a talebearer are as wounds, and they go down into the innermost parts of the belly.

Proverbs 26:22

CHAPTER SEVEN

Big Faith—
Big Life

Most people think of faith as believing in God. However, Satan knows there is a God, and he is well aware of Jesus. So clearly, faith is not just having the knowledge that God exists. Romans 12: 3 tells us, "God hath dealt to every man the measure of faith." It is the same measure that everybody receives when they ask Jesus to come into their heart. Sadly, most people do not develop their faith. They are ignorant of God's Word. Without the knowledge of the Word, one cannot grow and speak with the power and authority that Jesus says we have.

Those who put their faith in parents, education, money, psychiatrists or their earthly possessions eventually end up depressed. Such things as drugs, sex, food or shopping are used to try and fill the void that only God can fill. Putting your faith in anything or anybody other than God never relieves the pain of an empty soul. The dictionary defines faith as "belief, especially in a revealed religion; trust or reliance; a system of religious doctrines believed in; loyalty; pledged word."

God's Word says, "Faith is the substance of things hoped for, the evidence of things not seen" (Hebrews 11:1). Let's dissect this for clarity. *Faith is the substance* (something tangible) *of things hoped for* (things we want and pray for), *the evidence* (the reality) *of things not seen* (by the natural eye). Faith gives substance to our hopes, dreams and heartfelt desires that cannot be seen or understood with the natural mind's eye. For encouragement and the development of your faith, memorize what Jesus clearly said in Mark 11:23-24:

> *"For verily I say unto you, That whosoever shall say unto this mountain, Be thou removed, and be thou cast into the sea; and shall not doubt in his heart, but shall believe that those things which he saith shall come to pass; he shall have whatsoever he saith. Therefore I say unto you, what things soever ye desire, when you pray, believe that ye receive them, and ye shall have them."*

Faith, in the truest sense, is putting your complete trust in the Lord. With any issue you are facing, trust the Lord for the outcome. Put it into His hands and then let it go! The reason we do not receive the results prayed for is because most of the time, we do not let the problem go. As soon as we pray and give it to God, we say Amen (which means"so be it") -- but then we try to figure out how we are going to fix what we prayed for by ourselves. There is no faith involved if we are trying to control the outcome. Turning the situation over, means just that. DO NOT TAKE IT BACK! Your faith and relationship with Jesus will go to a new level when you get a hold of this principle.

> *Then touched He their eyes, saying, According to your faith be it unto you.*
>
> Matthew 9:29

Satan comes along and gives you a big dose of fear, which cancels out your faith. Doubt floods the mind with negative rhetoric dancing between your ears. Those are the times you must resist the devil and he will flee. Speak these paraphrased scriptures immediately:

> *"Above all, I take the shield of faith and I will quench the fiery darts of the wicked one."*
>
> Ephesians 6:16

> *"My God shall supply all my needs according to His riches in glory by Christ Jesus."*
>
> Philippians 4:19

"I will not be anxious for anything, but will pray about everything."

Philippians 4:6

"I will not fear, for God is with me, and He will strengthen me.."

Isaiah 41:10

Unwavering faith is a God-given gift—a gift for the asking. It is graciously given, so that we can learn to trust our Heavenly Father in every circumstance. Many times when we start to trust for something, like the rent that is due tomorrow, we give up and panic. First of all, panic is another form of fear. We are afraid that the rent will not be paid. We could possibly be evicted and then what would we do? God is known for showing up at the midnight hour, and He does, if we do not panic. Sometimes He waits until the last nanosecond, making it clear that He gets the glory —not us!

There are also times when God does not answer in the way that we are believing for. If we are not in obedience to His Word, He has no obligation to us. This reminds me of a story about a wonderful woman I once knew. She read the Bible for hours on end, fed the poor, gave generously to her church, and loved the Lord with all her heart. One day, she discovered that her bank account only had 23 cents in it. Everyone thought she had plenty of money because she shopped on a regular basis and gave generously to those around her. She had an abundance of clothes, purses and trinkets that filled her dresser drawers like a department store. When her rent was due, she exercised her faith by believing that the rent money would "supernaturally" appear. However, one day she was served with an eviction notice and was suddenly homeless and had to move in with friends. Satan had gotten into a vulnerable area in her life. She was in complete denial of her shopping addiction. She had some lessons to learn, as we all do.

A Lesson in Faith

This story that I'm about to share was the turning point in my understanding of faith and trust. During a road trip to do research for my book, *So...Help Me God*, supernatural experiences began to escalate. The gift of faith that I didn't even know existed, was about to befall me. As soon as my trip got underway, I watched everything begin to fall into place. People offered me places to stay and each contact led me to the next, without me even making a phone call. Soon it became evident that provision for every need that I had materialized within minutes.

I needed stamps—a woman said to me, "I went to the post office and bought stamps, and while I was there, I bought you some, too." I needed film for my camera —a stranger said, "I see you have a camera; I'm in the insurance business and I use a lot of film ... here -have a few rolls." I needed gas money to return to California—A lady who took me to lunch said, "I received a refund check today for something I had returned and I would like to contribute it for your research." Every aspect of that trip was taken care of.

When things flow like that, I truly believe that we are exactly where God wants us to be. However, the unthinkable was about to happen. On my way home to Los Angeles, as I was driving through Texas at two o'clock in the morning, my trusty Honda stopped dead. As I coasted to a very narrow shoulder of the road, I could not believe that God had allowed me to be stranded in the middle of nowhere in the dark of night. Semi-trucks were rolling by at high speeds and making my car rock back and forth. I remember thinking, *I must stay calm*. So I took my flashlight and signaled out the window, and soon a trucker stopped. He took my information and called AAA for me (this was before I had a cell phone).Shortly, the AAA truck came and towed me to the tiny town of Adrian, where there was one motel, a restaurant and a garage. However, they were all closed at that time of the morning.

The next day, the mechanic looked at my car and discovered that the timing chain had broken. Then he told me that he did not know how to fix Hondas, so I would have to be towed 100 miles back to Amarillo, Texas. Since I only had enough cash (no credit card back then) to get me home—I was stuck! The garage owner, who was also the mechanic as well as the AAA truck driver, wanted to call a tow truck for me, but I told him I had to think about it. He seemed a bit annoyed, wondering why I wasn't making a decision to take care of my dilemma.

As I sat there watching all the vehicles rush by on Interstate 40, I noticed a truck towing an empty flatbed behind it. Suddenly, I knew that a flatbed truck was the answer! So, I asked the mechanic if he knew someone who had a flatbed and could possibly help me. He replied, "No," becoming even more annoyed. Back in my car, I said, "Lord, I need a flatbed truck like the one I just saw." Within minutes, a yellow truck pulling an empty flatbed pulled up to the garage. Immediately, I knew it was mine. I don't know how I knew, I just knew!

The owners of the flatbed were a husband and wife from Santa Fe, New Mexico. They were on their way to Amarillo, when their water pump conked out. While the mechanic was repairing their water pump, we went to the restaurant. As God would have it, they were Christians. After we returned to the garage, they said, "Let's get this car (my Honda) up on here (their flatbed)."

Meanwhile, I phoned around looking for a mechanic in Amarillo. It was Saturday and most garages were closed. A Vietnamese mechanic told me to bring my car in to his place, so that is where they dropped me off. He told me that it would cost about $350 to fix it. *(Remember, I did not have the money for this.)* Interestingly, I was not led to tell Son Van Do (the mechanic), that I did not have any money.

After my flatbed showed up, I knew that God was showing me something through this situation. As Son worked on my Honda, I sat on an old sofa outside of the garage with my arms folded, quietly talking to God. I said, "God, I can't wait to see how You are going to do this." It was now after dark and my car was being put back together. I looked up and there was a sign on the wall that said, CASH ONLY— NO CHECKS. When it came time to pay the bill, Son said it was $100, instead of the originally quoted amount of $350. I looked him straight in the eyes and said, "You'll have to trust me."He never flinched as he said, "Okay." Then he proceeded to give me a new headlight, because one of mine was burned out, and he kept giving me things for my car until I drove away.

When I arrived in LA, I stopped at a friend's house to take a shower, and I told her my story. When I got out of the shower, there was an envelope by my purse with the money for the mechanic. That entire ordeal was financially taken care of. After that, I was never the same. I now know, that I know that I know, that God knows all of my needs without me telling anyone. He moves on the hearts of men and women, and choreographs every move to meet our needs.

FAITH IS TRUSTING GOD FOR EVERYTHING!

Faith Filled Words

Faith must be released through words. We know that the Scripture says that faith without *works* is dead, but faith without *words* is also dead. By our words, we ask Jesus into our heart. By words, we praise and worship Him. (When the praise goes up, the glory comes down!) Sometimes, just thinking the thought produces results. Romans 10: 9 says, "That if thou shalt confess with thy mouth the Lord Jesus, and shalt believe in thine heart that God hath raised Him from the dead, thou shalt be saved."

Notice, it says: CONFESS—WITH—THY—MOUTH. The mouth, the tongue, and the words that proceed out from them, are more powerful than a two-edged sword. Think about that when you criticize people with remarks such as "They've always been a drunk and they always will be," or "His dad was no good and neither is he." These words will curse those people, instead of blessing them. That would make you part of the problem instead of the solution. Speak faith-filled words like, "Your grace is sufficient to cover them; Lord protect and draw them to you, have mercy on them, Lord."

Since you will receive what you think and speak, it is wise to know the consequences of your desires. If you are a child of God who only wants God's best, then your desires will line up with the Word of God. You will want to be obedient to Biblical instruction. When you hear God's voice tell you to do something, you will gladly do it. There is always a blessing on the other side of what God asks of us. Sometimes when He asks us to sacrifice something, it's simply a test. The quicker we pass the test, the faster we go to a new level of faith.

When what we think or speak does not line up with the Word of God, then that becomes the devil's access point. It's the same as giving Satan a map directly to our money, our children, our bodies (health), and our emotions (fear and depression).

WRONG THINKING sends you to the world —
fueling self-centered desires that create unending misery.
RIGHT THINKING sends you to God —
giving life meaning, purpose, and unending peace.

The media has glamorized fame and fortune so much, that people of all ages hunger for it. Those who are invested in worldly careers who are not grounded in truth, usually find themselves on their knees crying "uncle." That's actually a good place to be—at the end of ourselves and our self-sufficiency. It's there that Daddy God can start to shape us and mold us for the purpose we were created for. I didn't say there was anything wrong with fame and fortune, just don't go seeking it.

If God opens the door for it, he will use it for His purposes. However, if you are struggling to make it happen and are desperate to be in the spotlight, take a look at your motives. The desire for money and popularity is nothing more than a temporary fix for underlying issues. Only Jesus can fill the void in your heart.

Refrain from putting your faith in a box, from putting yourself in a box, and from putting God in a box. Break out of the restraints and allow God to remove the shackles, and decide to be teachable to God's Word. God's Word is truth, and the truth will set you free, the truth will also grow your faith. The bigger your faith—the bigger your life!

PRAYER IS THE KEY TO HEAVEN,
BUT "FAITH" UNLOCKS THE DOOR!

Notes

Money Talk

"Rather go to bed supperless than rise in debt."

Benjamin Franklin

Money, or the lack of it, is the cause of most business disputes, marriage problems, crimes and depression. Although it is said that love makes the world go round, there is no doubt that money keeps it spinning. Most everything we do and everything we think we need has a price tag. Therefore, "I owe, I owe, it's off to work I go," is the average person's theme song. Unfortunately, most people are too busy making a living to make any money. Most people spend their entire lives chasing the almighty dollar in hopes of getting ahead. Some put their hope in the lottery or get-rich-quick schemes, because they don't see any other way to be able to live an abundant life.

Television and magazine ads continually pump out material messages in hopes that we will spend, spend, and then spend some more. We are encouraged to have bigger houses, better cars, fancier clothes, precious jewels, and exotic colognes to attract the ideal man or woman. Although "things" will never bring the happiness that we are told they will, money is still a necessity of life. There is nothing wrong with having money; it is the *love of money* that is the root of all evil (1 Timothy 6:10). Former Hollywood casting director, Mary Jo Slater once said, "Money is that dear thing, which if you're not careful, you can squander your whole life thinking of."

As prices skyrocket in the 21st century, we suddenly think we will have to cut back—thinking that there will not be enough cash to cover everything. Mistake # 1,—NEVER say, there is never enough! To the natural mind, this may be true; however, God has offered us an alternate financial route. God is our source, and He will provide. Provision is on its way the minute we call for it, when we trust God with unwavering faith. If one asks for provision, but prepares for lack, lack will prevail. The same goes for one who asks for success and prepares for failure—that person will also get what he has prepared for.

The United States and much of the world is in a fear-panic mode, as they watch their very foundations crumble.

If you are one of these people, snap out of it! Set your eyes upon Jesus! If you are putting your trust in Wall Street or what the evening news says, no wonder you are depressed. Put your trust in the only reliable "Source" in the entire universe—God Almighty. The Lord will guide you, give you wisdom, and provide supernaturally.

There are certain laws of responsibility concerning money that are placed on each of us. God tells us that we are only responsible for what has been made known to us; therefore, once we know a particular truth, we had better heed it. If we know that we should tithe to God's work, then we better tithe! When you think you cannot afford to tithe, that is when you need to tithe the most.

> ...he which soweth bountifully shall reap also bountifully.
>
> II Corinthians 9:6

Some Christians do not believe that tithing is for today because it is not mentioned in the New Testament. You are certainly not going to hell for not tithing. However, those who tithe can tell you that they notice a difference in their finances as a result of tithing. As a young girl, my Gramy once told me that if I would give faithfully to God, my needs would always be met. Showing God that you are taking Him at His Word will release a blessing. However, if you are avoiding the bill collectors and buying "things" before paying your debts or tithing, you cannot expect to be blessed. God does not want His children to be borrowers; He wants us to be debt-free. Think of Him as your financial advisor and business partner. Do not make any financial decisions without consulting Him.

Benjamin Franklin had it right when he said, "Debt hinders your freedom. Whoever you are in debt to has power over your liberty." When I first realized that God was putting it on my heart to be debt-free, I asked Him to help me. Soon I was offered two, good-paying jobs, doing what I loved. One was as a consultant for an entertainment company, and the other was marketing a family film. It felt good to pay my bills on time and watch my savings account grow. However, instead of paying off my debt, I was making sure that I had a nice cushion in the bank first.

When my jobs ended, I had money, but I was still in debt, even though the whole purpose of the financial blessing was to allow me to become debt-free. When my savings were used up, I still had debt. I goofed! Then God clearly revealed to me that if I would have paid off all of my debt, He would have continued to supply my finances. After telling God I was sorry, I asked for another chance. He didn't open any doors right away; in fact, I struggled financially for quite awhile after that. However, eventually I became debt-free.

The Lesson:

When we are immediately obedient to do what He is telling us, there is a blessing around the corner. When we procrastinate, we miss a blessing! As Mike Murdock says, "Delayed obedience is disobedience."

Give and it will be given unto you! The more generous you are, the more generous God is. He will prompt you how to give. Needs are all around us; however, none of us are called to fill every need we see. Pray before doling out the cash. It may seem like a good idea, but make sure it's God's idea and not yours. He will open the windows to your heavenly account when you are aligned with financial Kingdom principles—knowing what you should do and then doing it.

> *Bring ye all the tithes into the storehouse, that*
> *there may be meat in mine house, and prove me*
> *now herewith, saith the LORD of hosts, if I will not*
> *open you the windows of heaven, and pour you out*
> *a blessing, that there shall not be room enough to*
> *receive it.*
>
> Malachi 3:10

As God's children, our motives need to be rightly related to God's purposes. God tells us in Proverbs 28:27, "He that giveth unto the poor shall not lack: but he that hideth his eyes shall have many a curse." Psalm 41:1-2 says, "Blessed is he that considereth the poor: the LORD will deliver him in time of trouble. The LORD will preserve him, and keep him alive; and he shall be blessed upon the earth..."

God tells us that the poor will always be among us. There are families in dire need all around us and homeless folks who do not even know where they will lay their heads at night. Ask the Lord who you should help. God might put a ministry on your heart, or perhaps a missionary who needs support. When you are willing to be used financially, God will show you the need. Just be willing!

> *Give, and it shall be given unto you; good measure, pressed down, and shaken together, and running over, shall men give into your bosom. For with the same measure that ye mete withal it shall be measured to you again.*
>
> Luke 6:38

Ask—Believe—Receive

Those who continually say, "I can't afford it" are right, because they are speaking it into their circumstances. Reverse that mind set by saying: "There is no lack, for my God supplies all of my needs according to His riches in glory" (Philippians 4:19). Provision may not be tangible at the moment; however, it will be there when it is needed. All the gold and silver in and on the earth belongs to the Creator, so why are we fussing about it? He has given us

Biblical instruction —"Ask and it shall be given unto you." Pray, believing in your heart, and it shall come to pass. This is so simple that it is difficult for most people to grasp the concept and the absolute infallible truth of this. We listen to great preachers and teachers, but then we go about our everyday lives financially defeated. We know the truth and say we believe it, but until we apply God's Word and trust God wholeheartedly, then that wisdom is for naught.

It has been said, that we will not change anything we can tolerate. We also attract what we respect. Oil magnate, J. Paul Getty said, "People who do not respect money, don't have any." If you have a poverty mentality, then money will be difficult to come by and even harder to keep. Your thinking is locked into your small world of earnings from your job, social security, or disability.

In order to live your dreams and have a more abundant life, you must first know what you want—know your passion. Do what you love, using your God-given gifts, and the money will follow. Make the decision to break the back of poverty! Expect God to fulfill his promise, "Give and it will be given unto you." When you believe for provision, God will send people into your life to bless you financially, or He will give you a great idea that will generate income—perhaps a new job or a business venture. It could be a surprise check in the mail or an old inheritance that you didn't know you had coming. God deals with everyone differently. So NEVER try to figure out how it is coming—just know that it is on the way!

If you are helping to build God's kingdom and spreading the gospel, you are employed by God. God is good to His employees. He provides for everything that he calls us to do. Therefore, make sure it is God's idea—not your own.

When I wrote my first book, I told God that I needed a lot of money to publish it. Soon after that, I met a man who said, "God told me to publish your book." In short order, a team was formed for clerical and financial help. Everything I needed and more was at my fingertips. After the book came off the press, radio and TV interviews were prevalent Barnes and Noble took me on for book signings, and three visits to the White House ensued. Everyday I just went with the flow and continued to be in amazement throughout the whole process. You see, the book was God's idea; I was simply being obedient by writing it. What God orders, He pays for!

The Lord told thirty-eight parables in the gospels. Out of those thirty-eight, sixteen concern how we handle our money. There are also more than 2000 references to money and possessions throughout the Bible. God's Word is very clear on this issue, as can be seen in the books of Proverbs and Ecclesiastes. When we are good stewards of what we have, we will be entrusted with more. God's heavenly blessings enable us to take care of His earthly business.

Let's review this all-important topic:

1. Be aligned with financial "debt-free" Kingdom principles.

2. Be obedient to God's instruction concerning where your money should go.

3. When we are faithful with a little, we will be entrusted with much.

4. Be a cheerful and generous giver.

5. God blesses us financially to take care of His earthly business. It is our responsibility to do so!

GOD IS OUR SOURCE— NOT THE WORLD'S SYSTEM!

Notes

Talk Yourself Well

Regardless of today's advanced medical technology, people are sicker than ever. Prescription drugs line millions of medicine cabinets, yet people are not being healed.

There is no reason to die sick. You can absolutely live out your entire life with a healthy body. When you are healthy, you are rich! My grandmother said, "When you have your health, you have everything." Eat correctly, exercise, and trust God's Word for your health and vitality. This is in no way making light of those who have been maimed, crippled, or those who have been diagnosed with life-threatening diseases. Notice, I didn't say incurable diseases. Many doctors have given a death sentence to people who were later miraculously healed.

Norman Cousins said, "The first thing is that the will to live is not a theoretical abstraction, but a physiologic reality with therapeutic characteristics." When people asked him what he thought when he was told by specialists that his disease was progressive and incurable, he remarked, "The answer is simple, since I didn't accept the verdict, I wasn't trapped in the cycle of fear, depression, and panic that frequently accompanies a supposedly incurable illness."

Dr. Albert Schweitzer, who was a good friend of Norman Cousins, is another great example of encouragement. He knew that having a major purpose in life and a strong will to live acted as an energy force that keeps the body going. During an average day at his hospital in Lambarene,when he was in his 90's, he attended to his rounds, did strenuous carpentry, moved heavy crates of medicine, answered stacks of correspondence, worked on unfinished manuscripts, and played the piano. "I have no intention of dying" he once told his staff, "so long as I can do things. And if I do things, there is no need to die. So I will live a long, long time." And he did—until he was 95.

Most of the time, people die with their disease, because they believe there is no hope. When they give in to the "six months to live" report, the communication center of their brain prepares for the inevitable, causing their bodies to shut down. If you ever find yourself with a serious illness, decide that you are going to live and speak it out. "I will not die, but live and declare the works of the Lord" (Psalms 118:17).

If you enjoy living and you want to live a long fulfilling life—decide that you are going to live to be 120! "Your days shall be 120 years" (Genesis 6:3). Dr. Alexis Carrel, pioneer scientist of the Rockefeller Institute said, "There is no biological reason why human beings should not reach the age of 150."

Gramy's influence in my life was monumental, as you probably have surmised by the number of times that I have mentioned her. In grade school through high school, when the teacher would ask a question, I would raise my hand and start to answer by saying, "My Gramy said..." She started raising me when she was 50 years old. During this time, she was also taking correspondence classes in nursing, teaching ceramics, and helping to found a small church (she painted the picture of Jesus which hung behind the pulpit). She also played the piano, wrote several hymns, and even did flight testing for Piper Cub Aircraft during World War II.

My Gramy was definitely a tower of strength. At the age of 60, she started bowling and bowled for 30 more years— winning dozens of trophies. In her 80's, she was taking exercise classes at the YMCA, volunteering at the hospital, and delivering Meals-on-Wheels. She used to say, "These old people need their meals." She always had a smile for you and a helping hand if you needed one. The day she went to be with the Lord (at 92 years young), she was lifting cement blocks in her back yard. She came in the house for lunch, took a nap, and left her body.

Gramy's advice for staying young: "Don't sit down in that rocking chair or you're done!" There is much more that I could brag on about her, however, I just told you all this to encourage anyone who feels as if life has passed them by. It is never too late to do something! We become old because society tells us that at a certain age we become "seniors." We are then programmed for healthcare and told that we must have access to all the prescription drugs that we will obviously need, as we hobble off into retirement and prepare for the grave. Do not buy into that scenario! Search the scriptures for what God says about life and death. Throughout this book, there are scriptures that you can repeat until your heart and mind receive and believe them. Know that you are already healed, regardless of your symptoms. Thank God in advance for your healing, without doubting in your heart! Decide to live a healthy, productive life!

Disease and pain exist;however, according to God's Word, they do not have the right to continue in our bodies. Even though symptoms may hang on, do not give into the devil's doubts that bombard your mind. Satan comes to kill, steal and destroy. Laugh in his face and know that he has no power over you, unless you give it to him.

Disease is Only a Symptom, the Cause—Just a Thorn

Believers who say, "It is up to God if He wants to heal me," do not understand God's will or His ways. At one time, I thought the same way, until I studied the old-time spiritual leaders such as Smith Wigglesworth and read the work of Charles Capps. A whole new world opened up to me—what I was speaking was coming to pass! I came to understand that God gave us, His power and authority in Jesus' Name. His Word is power and authority, when we believe it and speak it!

When Jesus was on the cross, He said, "It is finished." Yes, He meant the plan of salvation was completed;however, He also literally meant, "IT IS FINISHED!" God is omnipotent, but He is not sitting on His throne manipulating puppet strings that are attached to our lives. He gave us His instruction manual for living—The Bible—wherein lies the answers to every healing need. In fact, the answer is there for every need we will ever encounter. Many people are perishing before their time because of their lack of Biblical knowledge. It breaks my heart to see people put their total faith in their doctor and a boatload of prescription drugs, without seeking God and His Word for healing.

My people are destroyed for lack of knowledge...

Hosea 4:6

My son, attend to my words; incline your ear to my
sayings. Let them not depart from your eyes; keep them
in the midst of your heart. For they are life unto those
that find them, and health to all their flesh.

Proverbs 4:20-22

Resist the temptation to talk about your illness, and especially resist any form of self-pity. Say, "Every day in every way I'm getting better and better. My immune system is stronger everyday. Praise You, Lord for supernatural health and energy." Talk to your body and tell it to line up with the Word of God. Speak to that area that is giving you trouble: "Liver be healed, I command you to function the way God created you to function. Thank You, Lord!" Do the same for any part of your body, including your mind (memory), your eyes (20-20 eyesight), ears (keen hearing), your muscles (firm and strong)—do it until you get results. UNBELIEF IS THE ONLY REASON OUR WORDS DO NOT MANIFEST!

As soon as you hear a negative thought or word come out of your mouth, put the gears of your mind in reverse. Verbally cancel those words or thoughts, and replace them immediately with positive affirmations. What we keep saying is what will manifest. The results could be immediate— a day, a week, or even months. DO NOT GIVE UP! The words that come out of your mouth can destroy you or release the life of God within you.

Death and life are in the power of the tongue.

Proverbs 18:21

Medical Findings

In Dr. David Yonggi Cho's book[3], *The Fourth Dimension*, he shared this:

One morning I was eating breakfast with one of Korea's leading neurosurgeons, who was telling me about various medical findings on the operation of the brain. He asked, "Dr. Cho, did you know that the speech center in the brain rules over all the nerves? You ministers really have power, because according to our recent findings in neurology, the speech center in the brain has total dominion over all the other nerves."

Dr. Cho (laughing): "I've known that for a long time."

Neurosurgeon: "How did you know that? In the world of neurology these are new findings."

Dr. Cho: "I learned it from Dr. James."

Neurosurgeon: "Who is this Dr. James?"

Dr. Cho: "He was one of the famous doctors in Biblical times, nearly two thousand years ago. And in his book, chapter three, the first few

---

[3]Dr. David Yonggi Cho, *The Fourth Dimension, Vol. 1*(Alachua: Bridge-Logos Publishers, 1979) Reprinted by permission from the publisher.

verses, Dr. James clearly defines the activity and importance of the tongue and the speech center."

Neurosurgeon (amazed): "Does the Bible really teach about this?"

Dr. Cho: "Yes. The tongue is the least member of our body, but can bridle the whole body."

Then this neurosurgeon began to expound their findings. He said that the speech nerve center had such power over all of the body, that simply speaking can give one control over his body, to manipulate it in the way he wishes.

He said, "If someone keeps on saying, 'I'm going to become weak,' then right away, all the nerves receive that message, and they say, 'Oh, let's prepare to become weak, for we've received instructions from our central communication that we should become weak.' They then, in natural sequence, adjust their physical attitudes to weakness."

He went on to say that if we say we can't do something, the nerves begin to declare the same thing, and the central nervous system receives that message, rendering the person incapable. This is the same for anything we say. So, don't say that you are old or you will definitely become ready for the grave.

Then the neurosurgeon expressed exactly what I had been thinking about the word "retirement." He said, "Once a man retires, he keeps repeating to himself, 'I am retired,' and all the nerves start responding and become less active, and ready for a quick death." There have been several people I knew, who constantly talked about their retirement, but never got a chance to enjoy it. My grandfather passed away the same year he retired, and he had never been sick.

Laughter Is Like a Medicine

A happy heart is good like medicine, and a cheerful mind works healing.

Proverbs 17:22

The "holy laughter" that entered the church a few years ago was very controversial, however, it reintroduced people to a very important emotion. People do not laugh nearly as much as they did in past years. As a nation, there is a crisis in the laughter department. The mood of the country has dampened our laughter and stripped our joy—and television programming hasn't helped. Do a TV fast from time to time and forego the news as much as possible. Unknowingly, people have become contaminated and desensitized by watching degrading television programs that our parents and grandparents would have considered unthinkable.

The body, soul, and spirit are being emotionally stimulated, either negatively or positively, every waking hour. What our ears and eyes are exposed to develops our character. Indulge yourself and your family with laughter and an uplifting environment. Happy, well-adjusted children grow into productive, happy adults and happy adults are healthier and more fun to be around.

As a teenager, my best friend Betty Harrow (who was voted class clown), constantly made me laugh. There were times when we laughed so hard at the after-school soda fountain, that fudge sundaes came out of my nose. Laughter was a big part of my life; therefore, I drew funny people to me. Early on, I found that comedy roles were my favorite to perform. In the late 70's, I won the title of "Ms. Unknown Comic" in Las Vegas at the Hacienda Hotel, while singing and dancing with a bag on my head. That gives you an idea of just how crazy this gal was!

However, around 2000-2001, I felt an unexplainable shift in my life, and a strange heaviness in the universe. It was a feeling like "the calm before the storm." Although I had the peace of God, there was an underlying sadness in my spirit and not much laughing going on. My life of joy, which had been filled with God's favor, was suddenly full of challenges. The good side of this was that I started to mature, and I have learned that there are different seasons we all go through—especially when the Lord is growing us up in Him and teaching us His ways.

Interestingly, I learned that I was not the only person who felt an eerie feeling at the start of the 21st century. It was like a subtle presence of evil. The news and the world scene rapidly changed for the worse. I'll just leave it at that—or this will turn into a political rant! Meanwhile, after reading about Norman Cousins, who was healed from an incurable disease by laughing, I was encouraged to laugh once again. His book *Anatomy of an Illness*, convinced me that laughter is a necessary emotion. Right then and there, I decided I wanted my laughter back—I was going to laugh more, even if I had to force myself.

I Love Lucy has always been my favorite TV show. Every chance I got, I tuned in to it and was immediately transported back to simpler times. If *I Love Lucy* wasn't on, then *The Andy Griffith Show* with crazy Don Knotts (Barney Fife) tickled my funny bone. The 50's sitcoms remind me of my happy childhood —always bringing a smile to my face. Recently my sister, Jo-Anna and my niece, Adina sent me the complete first season of *I Love Lucy* on DVD, so I'm good to go laugh!

In the past, when my mother, Jo-Anna, and I would get together, invariably one of us would say or do something to bring on a roaring laugh. Those side-splitting, uncontrollable fits of laughter would make us feel great! Something positive takes place during those delightful outbursts, when the stomach muscles are getting a real workout.

Research shows that laughter increases the body's flow of beneficial compounds and boosts its disease-fighting properties. It can be compared to an aerobic activity, as it increases the body's ability to utilize oxygen and the organs experience a type of internal "jogging." Laughter increases your immunity to infection by instantly increasing disease-fighting T-cells and B-cells, plus it releases proteins into the blood. Laughter also releases natural killer cells that destroy viruses and tumors, while also stimulating the heart and lungs. Natural pain killers are released, called endorphins, which are similar to morphine. Other benefits of laughter include stress reduction, lowered blood pressure, and a stronger immune system. So improve your health by having a hearty laugh at least once a day, with a few giggles thrown in for good measure.

LAUGHTER IS CONTAGIOUS—SPREAD IT AROUND!

My Miraculous Healing

In the 80's, I awoke one morning, unable to lift my arm. My first thought was that I had slept on it wrong. In a few days the stiffness went away; however, that was the first symptom of rheumatoid arthritis that eventually became full blown. Some days, my hands were not even flexible enough to pick up a toothbrush and my feet became so swollen that they could not fit into my shoes. A holistic doctor in Las Vegas told me not to give in to the arthritis by taking medication or Gold Shots. He encouraged me to eat brown rice and vegetables for seven years. Every seven years our bodies produce all new cells. He was actually telling me to eat a basic vegetarian diet. I have since learned that sickness of any kind will heal much quicker if we eat mostly raw fruits and vegetables, plus drink a lot of pure water. In addition to this, a sensible exercise program is vital—walking does wonders!

A few years later, a friend who watched me struggle with this arthritis insisted on taking me to a medical doctor in Los Angeles. Wanting to pacify my friend, I went. The doctor said, "You will have to live with this for the rest of your life." Immediately out of my mouth came the words, "No I won't!" My response surprised me because I didn't understand God's Word concerning healing at that time. What I did know, however, was that I was not willing to accept this crippling disease, even though I had struggled with it for approximately eight years.

One night, I attended a prayer meeting at Pastors Jim and Trish Steele's house, before they were pastors. As people were being prayed for, I mentioned my arthritis. One man said, "Let's pray for her right now." After Jim laid his hands on my head and prayed for my healing, he remarked how hot his hands had felt. In fact, he said his hands felt like they were on fire. Even though I didn't feel the heat, I knew that I had been healed! That was in the early 90's, and I have never had an arthritic symptom since then.

Once you experience supernatural healing, you can no longer deny that God heals. Jesus is the same yesterday, today, and forever. Since that time, I have witnessed many healings. Ironically, when I started writing this chapter on health, I became ill and my computer crashed. This time, blood work revealed a degenerative disease that was affecting every area of my body. Clearly, it was time to practice what I had been preaching. However, because I was weak and spent much of my time resting, I didn't always feel like speaking healing scriptures or talking myself well. My body was literally fighting to stay alive. During those times, we need others to cover us with prayer and do battle for us. Fortunately, I had faithful friends doing just that.

After eating a strict raw diet and juicing fruits and vegetables, my strength eventually returned. However, the symptoms were still evident and I continued talking about them. Then, one day, I heard in my spirit, "STOP TALKING SICK!" Immediately, I placed a sign saying just that on my desk. Reminding myself that I was a child of the Most High God, I decided right then and there that these symptoms were just that —symptoms! The Word says, "By His stripes I was healed," therefore, I am healed!

Those words—"STOP TALKING SICK"- were a major key! Even though I knew better, "sick" words came out of my mouth every time someone would ask, "How do you feel?" If you are sharing your ailments and are wondering why you are not receiving your healing, STOP IT NOW! Glory to God—I finally slapped my mouth into submission.

Is any sick among you? Let him call for the elders of the church; and let them pray over him, anointing him with oil in the name of the Lord: And the prayer of faith shall save the sick, and the Lord shall raise him up: and if he has committed sins, they shall be forgiven.

James 5: 14-15

Once we have been prayed for, there is no need to run to and fro seeking healing, or constantly asking for prayer. Know that it is a done deal! God got my attention when His still small voice asked, "Why are you chasing healing when healing is already yours?" Every day I sought remedies from homeopathic doctors and books while doing extensive research on the Internet concerning my symptoms. It was time to stop all that and rely solely on the guidance of the Holy Spirit. Most certainly, there is a place for exercise, nutrition, supplements, and yes, even doctors; however, becoming obsessed with any one of them can hinder the manifestation of healing. GOD IS OUR SOURCE—FOR EVERYTHING!

Take heed: Past emotional junk can—and will—hinder your healing. When people deny or push down anger, fear, guilt, shame, grief or the memories that caused these emotions, these emotions and memories become stored in their subconscious. Then their immune system reacts to these emotions and memories, as if they were still present. The

way a person acts and reacts on a daily basis is also deter-
mined by these past memories. All past negatives must be
dealt with, in order to obtain physical and emotional health.
You will know when a memory is fully processed because
you will feel completely free of any anger, grief, shame, fear,
guilt, pain or sadness attached to that particular memory.

I am the Lord that healeth thee.

Exodus 15:26

I can't emphasize enough to speak God's Word out loud.
Speak your desires out loud. Speak to God out loud. Think of
your body as the power plant and your mouth as the switch!

Rise up and be healed in the name of Jesus! Hallelujah!

For healing, read aloud the following Gos-Pill Capps-
sules[4] three times a day, (paraphrased to fit you personally).
Memorize them! Meditate on them until they are part of
your very soul—until they are second nature to you, as
much as breathing is to staying alive.

> *"Christ has redeemed me from the curse of the law.
> Therefore, I forbid any sickness or disease to come-
> upon this body. Every disease germ and virus that
> touches this body dies instantly, in the name of Jesus.*[5]

---

[4] The phrase "Gos-Pill Capps-sules" was coined by Charles Capps in *The Tongue A Creative Force.*

[5] Charles Capps, *The Tongue: A Creative Force.* (England, Arkansas: Capps Publishing, 1976). Reprinted by permission of the publisher.

Every organ and every tissue of this body functions in the perfection to which God created it to function, and I forbid any malfunction in this body, in the name of Jesus." [6]

> Galatians 3:13; Romans 8:11;
> Genesis 1:30; Matthew 16: 19

"I take the shield of faith and I quench every fiery dart that the wicked one brings against me." [7]

> Ephesians 6:16

"No weapon formed against me shall prosper, for my righteousness is of the Lord. But whatever I do will prosper for I'm like a tree that's planted by the rivers of water."[8]

> Isaiah 54:17; Psalm 1:3

"I will fear no evil for thou art with me Lord, your Word and your Spirit they comfort me." [9]

> Psalm 23:4

"I am an overcomer and I overcome by the blood of the lamb and the word of my testimony." [10]

> Revelation 12:11

---

6 Ibid
7 Ibid
8 Ibid
9 Ibid
10 Ibid page 97

"I present my body to God for it is the temple of the LIVING GOD. God dwells in me and HIS LIFE permeates my SPIRIT, SOUL and BODY so that I am filled with the fullness of God Daily"[11]

Romans 12:1-2; John 14:20

"You have forgiven all my iniquities; You have healed all my diseases; You have redeemed my life from destruction; You have satisfied my mouth with good things so that my youth is renewed like the eagles." [12]

Psalm 103:2-5

"My immune system grows stronger day by day. I speak life in my immune system. I forbid confusion. The same Spirit that raised Christ from the dead dwells in me and quickens my immune system with life and the wisdom of God, guarding the life and health of my body."[13]

Romans 8:11

I shall not die but live and declare the works of God.[14]

Psalm 118:17

---

11 Capps, Charles, **God's Creative Power© for Healing.** (England, Arkansas: Capps Publishing, 1991). Reprinted by permission of the publisher
12 Ibid
13 Ibid
14 Ibid

Regardless of how you feel, confess the promises of the Lord, and they will manifest unto you!

(NOTE: In the back of the book, you will find 101 things God Said About Healing. Highlight the ones that speak to you.)

Notes

CHAPTER TEN

Receive Supernaturally

Now that you have grasped the power of the spoken word, it's time to put it into practice and start receiving supernaturally. In a minute, I will lay out a simple plan that will help you accomplish your goals. First, this point must be made—"... seek ye first the kingdom of God, and his righteousness; and all these things shall be added unto you" (Matthew 6:33). My Gramy told me many times that I needed to put God first. Since I already believed in God, I didn't know what she was trying to tell me—until I had a born-again experience while watching The 700 Club with Pat Robertson. It felt like lightning came through the roof and zapped me! I wept for what seemed like hours. Immediately after the tears stopped, I thought differently, saw differently, and my heart felt differently. My first thought was, *That's what Gramy meant!*

In an instant, God became "Number One" in my life. *"Seek Ye First the Kingdom of God,"* has become my signature scripture. If I was prone to tattoos, I would have it tattooed on my forehead. It's not just enough to accept Jesus as Savior. He needs to be the Lord of our lives—the boss! Trust God with every detail of your life; don't make a decision without Him. Love Him with all of your heart and develop a personal relationship with Him. Have a love affair with your Bible.

Of course, we can go on our merry way and do whatever we want without involving God. He gave us a free-will to make our own decisions. However, ignoring the God of the universe comes with a high price tag, as America is finding out. When we see ungodly people who seem to have it all, they rarely do—in fact they don't! Most of them end up in pathetic scenarios. To be apart from the Father is a scary place to be! The world system has nothing to offer. We were made by God, for God. The only things that are permanent and meaningful are the things that we do for Christ. The goal for our lives is to fulfill our God-given purpose during the short time we have on earth.

With that said, here is the foolproof "Supernatural Plan" that will bring forth your heart's desires.

> *Delight yourselves in the Lord; and He will give you the desires of your heart.*
>
> Psalm 37:4

The Supernatural Plan

Write the vision, and make it plain upon tables, that he may run that readeth it.

Habakkuk 2:2,3

1. Write down what you want.
2. Read the list three times a day.
3. Do not talk to anyone about your plan, except God.

It's that simple!

Write down what you want. Make a list of the things you want materially, physically, or spiritually. The list will change from time to time, as your priorities change.

Read the list three times a day. Read it out loud morning, noon and night thinking of your desires often. Feel the finality of already acquiring those things. Get excited in your spirit. See those things as already being in your possession.

Do not talk to anyone about your plan except God. If you do, it gives others the chance to think or speak negatively against what you are believing for. All speech has power; therefore, you do not want anyone's negativity to interfere.

Important: Do not waste time trying to figure out how your list will manifest. Wipe away any doubts. Let God bring it. Having money or education has nothing to do with you receiving supernaturally. If you find it difficult to believe for the bigger things, start with smaller things.

VERY IMPORTANT: Make sure your goals are not to the detriment of anyone. May the manifestation of your desires be glorifying to God. Thank God in advance for the things that are supernaturally on the way, and be careful what you ask for! Some desires on your list may manifest quickly, while others will take more time.

PERSISTENCE WINS OUT!

Start your list now...
...and start receiving supernaturally!

Immediate Goals

1._____

_____

_____

_____

_____

2._____

_____

_____

_____

_____

3._____

_____

_____

_____

_____

4._____

_____

_____

_____

_____

5._____

_____

_____

_____

6._____

_____

_____

_____

_____

7._____

_____

_____

_____

_____

8._____

_____

_____

_____

_____

9._____

_____

_____

_____

_____

10._____

_____

_____

_____

_____

Long-Term Goals

1._____
_____
_____
_____
_____

2._____
_____
_____
_____
_____

3._____
_____
_____
_____
_____

4._____
_____
_____
_____
_____

5._____
_____
_____
_____

6._____

_____

_____

_____

7._____

_____

_____

_____

_____

8._____

_____

_____

_____

9._____

_____

_____

_____

10._____

_____

_____

_____

_____

THINK SUPERNATURALLY

BELIEVE SUPERNATURALLY

DREAM SUPERNATURALLY

GIVE SUPERNATURALLY

FORGIVE SUPERNATURALLY

LOVE SUPERNATURALLY

RECEIVE SUPERNATURALLY

Notes

God's Will to Heal

Keith Moore

God Said So!

How do we know whether it's God's will to heal us or not? It makes little difference what others say about it. What did He say about it? Remember that God is no respecter of persons (Acts 10:34), and He never changes (Malachi 3:6). So what He said to them yesterday, He is saying to you today. God's Word is God speaking to me.

(The following statements are taken directly from the Bible with little or no variation. The verbs and construction have been changed to apply to you personally and to sum up the thoughts in some instances. Also, many of these statements are prefaced by phrases like, "If you walk in My commandments,""If you believe ... obey ...." etc.)

What did God say? Let's look at 101 Things God Said..

101 Things God Said

Old Testament

God said ...

1) *I am the Lord that healeth thee* (Exodus 15:26).

2) *Your days shall be one hundred and twenty years* (Genesis 6:3).

3) *You shall be buried in a good old age* (Genesis 15:15).

4) *You shall come to your grave in a full age, like as a shock of corn cometh in his season* (Job 5:26).

5) *When I see the blood, I will pass over you and the plague shall not be upon you to destroy you* (Exodus 12:13).

6) *I will take sickness away from the midst of you and the number of your days I will fulfill* (Exodus 23:25,26).

7) *I will not put any of the diseases you are afraid of on you, but I will take all sickness away from you* (Deuteronomy 7:15).

8) *It will be well with you, and your days shall be multiplied and prolonged as the days of heaven upon the earth* (Deuteronomy 11:9,21).

9) *I turned the curse into a blessing unto you, because I loved you* (Deuteronomy 23:5 and Nehemiah 13:2).

10) *I have redeemed you from every sickness and every plague* (Deuteronomy 28:61 and Galatians 3:13).

11) *As your days, so shall your strength be* (Deuteronomy 33:25).

12) *I have found a ransom for you, your flesh shall be fresher than a child's and you shall return to the days of your youth* (Job 33:24,25).

13) *I have healed you and brought up your soul from the grave; I have kept you alive from going down into the pit* (Psalm 30:1,2).

14) *I will give you strength and bless you with peace* (Psalm 29:11).

15) *I will preserve you and keep you alive* (Psalm 41:2).

16) *I will strengthen you upon the bed of languishing; I will make all your bed in your sickness* (Psalm 41:3).

17) *I am the health of your countenance and your God* (Psalm 43:5).

18) *No plague shall come near your dwelling* (Psalm 91:10).

19) *I will satisfy you with long life* (Psalm 91:16).

20) *I heal all your diseases* (Psalm 103:3).

21) *I sent My word and healed you and delivered you from your destructions* (Psalm 107:20).

22) *You shall not die, but live, and declare My works* (Psalm 118:17).

23) *I heal your broken heart and bind up your wounds* (Psalm 147:3).

24) *The years of your life shall be many* (Proverbs 4:10).

25) *Trusting Me brings health to your navel and marrow to your bones* (Proverbs 3:8).

26) *My words are life to you, and health/medicine to all your flesh* (Proverbs 4:22).

27) *(My) good report makes your bones fat* (Proverbs 15:30).

28) *(My) pleasant words are sweet to your soul and health to your bones* (Proverbs 16:24).

29) *My joy is your strength. A merry heart does good like a medicine* (Nehemiah 8:10; Proverbs 17:22).

30) *The eyes of the blind shall be opened. The eyes of them that see shall not be dim* (Isaiah 32:3; 35:5).

31) *The ears of the deaf shall be unstopped. The ears of them that hear shall hearken* (Isaiah 32:3; 35:5).

32) *The tongue of the dumb shall sing. The tongue of the stammerers shall be ready to speak plainly* (Isaiah 35:6; 32:4).

33) *The lame man shall leap as a hart* (Isaiah 35:6).

34) *I will recover you and make you to live. I am ready to save you* (Isaiah 38:16,20).

35) *I give power to the faint. I increase strength to them that have no might* (Isaiah 40:29).

36) *I will renew your strength. I will strengthen and help you* (Isaiah 40:31; 41:10).

37) *To your old age and gray hairs I will carry you and I will deliver you* (Isaiah 46:4).

38) *I bore your sickness* (Isaiah 53:4).

39) *I carried your pains* (Isaiah 53:4).

40) *I was put to sickness for you* (Isaiah 53:10).

41) *With My stripes you are healed* (Isaiah 53:5).

42) I will heal you (Isaiah 57:19).

43) Your light shall break forth as the morning and your health shall spring forth speedily (Isaiah 58:8).

44) I will restore health unto you, and I will heal you of your wounds saith the Lord (Jeremiah 30:17).

45) Behold I will bring health and cure, and I will cure you and will reveal unto you the abundance of peace and truth (Jeremiah 33:6).

46) I will bind up that which was broken and will strengthen that which was sick (Ezekiel 34:16).

47) Behold, I will cause breath to enter into you and you shall live. And I shall put My Spirit in you and you shall live (Ezekiel 37:5,14).

48) Whithersoever the rivers shall come shall live. They shall be healed and every thing shall live where the river comes (Ezekiel 47:9).

49) Seek Me and you shall live (Amos 5:4,6).

50) I have arisen with healing in My wings (beams) (Malachi 4:2).

New Testament

51) *I will, be thou clean* (Matthew 8:3).

52) *I took your infirmities* (Matthew 8:17).

53) *I bore your sicknesses* (Matthew 8:17).

54) *If you're sick you need a physician. (I am the Lord your physician)* (Matthew 9:12 & Exodus 15:26).

55) *I am moved with compassion toward the sick and I heal them* (Matthew 14:14).

56) *I heal all manner of sickness and all manner of disease* (Matthew 4:23).

57) *According to your faith, be it unto you* (Matthew 9:29).

58) *I give you power and authority over all unclean spirits to cast them out, and to heal all manner of sickness and all manner of disease* (Matthew 10:1 & Luke 9:1).

59) *I heal them all* (Matthew 12:15 & Hebrews 13:8).

60) *As many as touch Me are made perfectly whole* (Matthew 14:36).

61) *Healing is the children's bread* (Matthew 15:26).

62) *I do all things well. I make the deaf to hear and the dumb to speak* (Mark 7:37).

63) *If you can believe, all things are possible to him that believeth* (Mark 9:23; 11:23,24).

64) *When hands are laid on you, you shall recover* (Mark 16:18).

65) *My anointing heals the brokenhearted and delivers the captives, recovers sight to the blind and sets at liberty those that are bruised* (Luke 4:18; Isaiah 10:27; 61:1).

66) *I heal all those who have need of healing* (Luke 9:11).

67) *I am not come to destroy men's lives but to save them* (Luke 9:56).

68) *Behold, I give you authority over all the enemy's power and nothing shall by any means hurt you* (Luke 10:19).

69) *Sickness is satanic bondage and you ought to be loosed today* (Luke 13:16 & II Corinthians 6:2).

70) *In Me is life* (John 1:4).

71) *I am the bread of life. I give you life* (John 6:33,35).

72) *The words I speak unto you are spirit and life* (John 6:63).

73) *I am come that you might have life, and that you might have it more abundantly* (John 10:10).

74) *I am the resurrection and the life* (John 11:25).

75) *If you ask anything in My name, I will do it* (John 14:14).

76) *Faith in My name makes you strong and gives you perfect soundness* (Acts 3:16).

77) *I stretch forth My hand to heal* (Acts 4:30).

78) *I, Jesus Christ, make you whole* (Acts 9:34).

79) *I do good and heal all that are oppressed of the devil* (Acts 10:38).

80) *My power causes diseases to depart from you* (Acts 19:12).

81) *The law of the Spirit of life in Me has made you free from the law of sin and death* (Romans 8:2).

82) *The same Spirit that raised Me from the dead now lives in you and that Spirit will quicken your mortal body* (Romans 8:11).

83) *Your body is a member of Me* (I Corinthians 6:15).

84) *Your body is the temple of My Spirit and you're to glorify Me in your body* (I Corinthians 6:19,20).

85) *If you'll rightly discern My body which was broken for you and judge yourself, you'll not be judged and you'll not be weak, sickly or die prematurely* (I Corinthians 11:29-31).

86) *I have set gifts of healing in My body* (I Corinthians 12:9).

87) *My life may be made manifest in your mortal flesh* (II Corinthians 4:10,11).

88) *I have delivered you from death, I do deliver you, and if you trust Me, I will yet deliver you* (II Corinthians 1:10).

89) *I have given you My name and have put all things under your feet* (Ephesians 1:21,22).

90) *I want it to be well with you and I want you to live long on the earth* (Ephesians 6:3).

91) *I have delivered you from the authority of darkness* (Colossians 1:13).

92) *I will deliver you from every evil work* (II Timothy 4:18).

93) *I tasted death for you. I destroyed the devil who had the power of death. I've delivered you from the fear of death and bondage* (Hebrews 2:9, 14,15).

94) *I wash your body with pure water* (Hebrews 10:22; Ephesians 5:26).

95) *Lift up the weak hands and the feeble knees. Don't let that which is lame be turned aside but rather let Me heal it* (Hebrews 12:12,13).

96) *Let the elders anoint you and pray for you in My name and I will raise you up* (James 5:14,15).

97) *Pray for one another and I will heal you* (James 5:16).

98) *By My stripes you were healed* (I Peter 2:24).

99) *My divine power has given unto you all things that pertain unto life and godliness through the knowledge of Me* (II Peter 1:3).

100) *Whosoever will, let him come and take of the water of life freely* (Revelation 22:17).

101) *Beloved, I wish above all things that you may...be in health* (III John 2).

Copied with permission from Faith Life Church,
Branson, Missouri.

Notes

God's Guarantee

If you believe in Jesus, but do not have a personal relationship with Him, ask Jesus into your heart to be the Lord of your life. Ask for forgiveness for the past "junk" that was not pleasing to Him (He wipes the slate clean as if those things never happened). Say, "Use me Lord, take my life and do something with it." Surrender!

> *Whosoever shall call on the name of the Lord shall be saved.*
>
> Acts 2:21

> *If thou shalt confess with thy mouth the Lord Jesus, and shalt believe in thine heart that God hath raised Him from the dead, thou shalt be saved.*
>
> Romans 10:9

The Holy Spirit will come to live within you. Ask, and the Holy Spirit will give you the ability to speak with other tongues. (Luke 11:13; Acts 2:4).

For anyone doubting the existence of God, there is a God! A God who loves you! The God who breathed the breath of life into you! The Creator of the universe is waiting for you with open arms. Meet His Son Jesus, the Savior who died on the cross for the sins of the world and for you and me, so that we may have eternal life with our heavenly Father. With a sincere heart ask, or scream if you need to, "If You're real, show me!" Use your own words and diligently seek Him. If you do this and sincerely want to know the truth, you will meet the Truth face-to-face.

"I am the way, the truth, and the life: no one comes to the Father, but by me."

John 14:6

You shall know the truth and the truth shall make you free.

John 8:32

KWITCHURBELYAKIN

Words are the most powerful things in the universe

If you can't say anything good – shut up

Talk yourself well

Cursing or blessing is on your tongue

Highly charged "negative" words electrocute the soul

Uplifting "positive" words renew the soul

Reaping what you sow is spiritual law

Big faith, big life

Encourage yourself and others with happy talk

Life and death are in the power of the tongue

Your tongue determines your destiny

Adversity is the breakfast of champions

Kick the negative habit

Idle chatter – idle life

Never say can't

7 Days to Greatness

NOTE: Now that you have learned about the "power of words," the following pages will give you more food for thought—helping you to achieve a higher level of living. You will learn how to become free to accomplish great things. Get ready to prepare your Body to be healthy, your Soul to be happy, and a Holy Spirit that will lead you to greatness!

Introduction

The word "greatness" can mean different things to different people. Taking that in to consideration, I believe that when you follow through on the assignments in this book you *will* discover *your* "greatness." The BODY, SOUL and SPIRIT must operate in unison. When the three are balanced, life works! The goal is for the BODY to be HEALTHY, the SOUL to be HAPPY(content), and the SPIRIT—HOLY.

When I was about 20 years old I read the book How to Stay Young and Vital by Bob Cummings. It made an everlasting impression—teaching me how to have a healthy **BODY**. To this day I cannot figure out why I was reading that book at such a young age. A friend in California once remarked that I was health conscious before it was fashionable.

Being fit physically and emotionally is vital if we are going to accomplish what we are called to do. Before the modern day health craze emerged, God had already given us instructions how to be healthy and happy in His (health) Book. God is the original Fitness King!

Eating nutritious food and a bit of exercising is wise, but obsessing over it could be a distraction. Wanting to be physically attractive also takes up time. Just ask me! Looking in the mirror, while holding up my face to see what I could look like with a face lift, wastes valuable time. Perhaps I need to be set free of that!

The **SOUL,** being our *mind, will* and *emotions,* usually needs the most work. FREEDOM from past emotional junk will allow a person to soar like an eagle. Fortunately, I was not a troubled child, and I never did drugs or had self-destructive tendencies as many in the entertainment field have had to deal with. However, my focus was a self-centered career. The only thing that was important to me was Show Business—it was my God. Michael Jackson once said that when he was performing on stage was when he felt complete, that's how I felt—until I met Jesus!

Our minds rationalize everything we do, to justify what we do. Our stubborn "will" alienates the people that can help us the most, and our sensitive emotions can be so stuck in the past that we ruin every relationship and opportunity that comes our way. All these natural in-the-flesh negatives will create chaos and unhappiness for a life time, until they are dealt with—which you are about to do!

For the most part, we are all a bit selfish. Especially if we only think about what makes us happy, and forgetting about the happiness of others. To find your greatness, selfishness will have to go! It is safe to say that most selfish people don't realize that they are selfish. I didn't! When the baggage we carry around from the past is dealt with, our hearts become softer and less selfish. God will do heart surgery on our hardened hearts when we allow Him to. Throw your pride to the wind!

The **SPIRIT** that dwells in us determines our quality of life and our eternal future. Our spiritual walk, habits, friends, and our environment will determine what kind of spirit we carry around. Of course, if you are acquainted with the God who created you, then you are already walking toward greatness. If you do not have a clue what I'm talking about—stay tuned! There are no grey areas; we are either living in the light or walking in darkness.

If you apply what you are about to read, you will discover freedom in every area of your life—eliminating worry, fear, unworthiness, and those issues that may have been holding you back in life. All you are required to do at this very moment is to decide to be open to God's truth. Be willing to take the steps that will help lead you to the divine-purpose you were created for.

God created the world in six days and rested on the seventh. So we know a lot can be done in a week's time. The Bible says that a day is like a thousand years to God, however, don't let that throw you. Life on planet earth is set up for a seven day week, so let's stick with that. We are created in the image of God and we have been given power and authority to "Call things that are not in to being" by using the name of Jesus. The name of Jesus carries POWER! We are co-heirs with Jesus! Digest this: We are co-heirs with the SON of GOD! Now let's get busy!

Healthy Body

THE BODY: is the temple of the Holy Spirit, given by God and bought with a price—therefore we are not our own—as explained in 1Corinthians 6: 19-20. We can liken our bodies to a vessel or a container that houses the Kingdom of God (Luke 17:21). One day when our heart stops, that will be the end of the body—but not the end of you and me. Regardless of the number of years we may live on earth, we are going to live in eternity forever and ever, and ever, which is an incomprehensible length of time—in fact time doesn't exist in eternity! Therefore, I want to be prepared for where I am going to live FOREVER! Our short time on earth is a school of preparation for our eternal home. Let's POWER-UP and do life the way God meant it to be.

God created us and breathed the breath of life into us for His purpose. Therefore, life will not work or make sense until we understand that. We were given free will, but when we go about out own lives doing as we please without God's covering, we invariably mess up. When we consult the Word of God and the Holy Spirit for direction in all we do, life flows the way it was designed to.

The body lives and breathes as long as our heart keeps beating and the blood keeps flowing. "For the life of the flesh is in the blood: (Leviticus 17:11) Under certain circumstances we are quite fragile and can be crushed like a bug. At other times we are tough as nails—surviving all odds. We human body beings are remarkable creatures. We come in all sizes and colors and in the grand scheme of things—we populate the world! And… if we want to enjoy this life we must be in good health.

The inner workings of the physical body can be complicated and confusing. However, God reveals in His Word how to stay healthy and how to treat our bodies. There is no guess work! When it comes to health issues, many of us turn to vitamin supplements and fad diets that bombard us on a regular basis—leaving us wondering: What ones are the best—do they work—are they worth the money? My five years of health challenges gave me a priceless education that I'm excited to share with you.

I thought I knew all about eating right and doing what was best for my health. However, I ignored the fact that eating a pint of Hagen Daz ice cream (on occasion), plus drinking coffee lattes, was not the best nutritional plan. When I found myself in a life or death situation, I knew I had to get serious about what I was putting in my body. My immune system needed strengthened. It is suspected that my immune system was compromised by mold from a water leak in my house. If you have signs of mold in your living environment it needs dealt with immediately—it can be lethal!

A few years ago, God put it on my heart to tell Believers that it is time to build their immune systems. This message was in the form of a warning: *"Perilous times are coming. You might need to escape a situation that will require running or moving quickly. Your life may depend on your physical condition."* Satan is inflicting disease and pain on thousands of Christians—aiming to kill, steal, and destroy. Decide to take action NOW! Strengthen your bodies the best you can, and be ready for battle at a moments notice. Be strong in the Lord, physically and spiritually! Do not let your guard down—put on the full armor of God every morning (Ephesians 6:10-18). No one can put on the armor for you.

Putting on the armor is a decision to put on Jesus, so that you can go forth in His strength victoriously, regardless of the battle you are confronted with.

Part of the battle is the average American diet which consists of over-cooked processed foods, meat and dairy injected with carcinogenic hormones, and the killer, sugar (read *Sugar Blues*). Masses of people are fighting vitamin and mineral deficiencies and are not aware of it. Most disease is related to deficiencies or fungus. When the immune system is compromised, the body can no longer fight off bacteria and viruses—causing sickness and disease. And…no prescription drug will fix it.

Give the body what it needs and it will heal! It is not easy these days to find nutritious uncompromised food. It is either sprayed with pesticides, been Genetically Modified (GMO), or been sitting in a warehouse for long periods of time—reducing the vitamin and mineral content. However, in the summer you can grow a garden or shop at your local Farmers Market. In the winter, you will make sure to add vitamin supplements and look for organic fruits and vegetables—frozen veggies will work also. There are many opinions concerning supplements, so you must do your homework. There are hundreds, probably thousands of nutritional books on the market. Therefore, I am not going to attempt to recommend a health regimen; however, I will share the basics that restored my health.

If you recall, I was on my death bed with my internal organs shutting down. First of all, I decided I was not going to die. Food wise I stopped eating dead food, which is anything cooked, packaged, or processed. If it came in a box or a can I didn't even consider it. Fresh vegetables eaten raw and juiced became my diet for about two years, and still is a vital part of my health routine. I eliminated ALL sugar including fruit. Now I eat fruit, but I don't over do it. My immune system and my strength were restored. I also took Standard Process supplements, which are plant based, and are only available through Chiropractors and Kineseologists. And…I fixed my eyes and my heart on the healing scriptures, reading them out loud until I knew that I knew I was healed—regardless of symptoms.

NOTE: I didn't entertain traditional medicine because drugs don't cure, they simply mask the problem. God's word is medicine: "Attend to my words…they are life…and health to all their flesh" (Proverbs 4:20-22).

This may seem quite radical to some, however, if you are sick or have been fighting a fatal disease you can recover if you starve the sickness. Sugar, carbohydrates, meat and dairy products feed disease. I'm speaking from experience! It takes discipline and making the decision that you are going to win the battle! When we give into a particular diagnosis and lose hope, we will go down hill fast. Remember to take the healing scriptures to heart and thank God for your healing in advance. Review Chapter nine: Talking Yourself Well.

NOTE: Some healings are instant, which I call miracles, others are progressive.

Poor health takes years to overtake the body and it can take a year or more to heal. Fortunately, God designed the body to heal itself. However…we can't continue to eat dead food and expect to get well. Below are 10 vital common sense basics for healthy living.

1. Drink plenty of good filtered water everyday— half your weight in ounces. Dehydration is a common and serious problem.

2. Move every day—stretch, walk, swim, jump on a trampoline (circulation is vital).

3. Deep breathing is one of the keys to healthy living—expanding the lungs and giving the brain cells the much needed oxygen. Instead of an energy drink, go outside, breath deep, and hold it as long as you can, then slowly blow it out—repeat several times.

4. Eat plenty of raw leafy green vegetables—fruits and colored veggies as well.

5. Keep the bowels and intestines flushed out!!!!!!!!

6. 15 minutes of morning sun for essential vitamin D (no sunblock—statistics show that there is more skin cancer since the use of sunblocks).

7. Hydrotherapy—hot and cold showers & hot Epsom salt baths releases toxins.

8. Give up negative TV—including the news.

9. Eliminate clutter

10. Stand tall, walk briskly and greet everyone with a smile.

Foods to Avoid:

1. SUGAR—all commercial snacks, deserts, soda's and energy drinks. Sugar is in most packaged and canned foods. Beware: Evaporated cane juice is sugar! Most artificial sweeteners are poisonous to the body. Stevia is acceptable— after you are healed raw honey and pure maple syrup are healthy choices.

2. Meats and poultry that are not organically raised. Soy and corn is the main diet for beef and chickens because it is cost affective. The corn is GMO and soy is not fit for human consumption, especially for men. Whatever the animal eats—we are consuming—including the eggs.

3. Commercial dairy products—they contain fillers as well as sugar.

4. Fast food!!!!!!!!!!!!!!!!!

5. Grains with gluten. Wheat was a staple in the Bible. However, I have come to believe that those that think they are allergic to gluten may not really be allergic to the wheat, barley, rye and other grains—it may well be the many pesticides that are sprayed in excess on them. Those pesticides and preservatives play havoc

with the digestive track, stomach and intestines.

These basic rules apply when restoring your health and for living a healthy lifestyle. If this information is new to you, you will soon learn that there are many diverse opinions, so read, and pray, for what is best for you. Get in the habit of "reading labels." If a label has words that you can't pronounce, put it back on the shelf!

Jesus heals! However, it is our responsibility to give the body the nutrition it needs. The Bible has given us clear instructions on God's way of eating. There was no processed food in the Garden of Eden! There were also no poisons applied to nature's food. Do yourself and your family a life saving favor and learn about clean, healthy eating. Jordan S. Rubin, of the Maker's Diet, is one source of acceptable and forbidden foods, as written in Leviticus Chapter 11.

Pray over your food: "Thank you Lord for blessing and sanctifying this food for the nourishment of my body. I'm grateful for my daily food—thank you Father." Many times I hold my hands over my food when I pray. Energy is emitted from our hands. If you have a personal relationship with the Holy Spirit you are carrying the anointing of Jesus in your hands.

Our inherited DNA determines our height, color of hair and eyes, our complexion, and sometimes our weight and health. However, with proper nutrition and exercise, the body has the ability to change course and improve any particular condition. Your temple is the creation of your heavenly Father, treat it with Tender Loving Care.

If you had a doctor that had a prescription that was totally natural and it could guarantee good health for your entire life would you want it? There is such a drug! It enhances your immune system and every cell in your body and your brain. As you may be aware, the immune system continually fights germs, cancer cells, and every ill that may attack the body. Our modern-day world is loaded with pollutants that will hinder immune fighting properties. However, negative emotions like guilt, sadness, anger and grief also suppress immune response—triggering brain chemicals that will eventually prove dangerous to the body and the brain. This is why it is vital to work through "emotional junk" by the renewing of the mind—discussed in the next section.

The prescription for the most powerful Miracle Drug available is: JOY & LAUGHTER! Find your "happy-place" and do your "happy dance" The Bible tells us that the JOY of the Lord is our strength (Nehemiah 8:10). I encourage you to take this literally!

NOTE: Protect your immune system so it can protect you!

Happy Soul

THE SOUL: is made up of your MIND, WILL, and EMOTIONS. The soul thinks acts and reacts to given situations, this side of heaven. To have a Happy Soul we must be emotionally healthy. Unfortunately the perils of life (abuse, loss, rejection, betrayal, shame, etc.) contribute to a restless and troubled soul. Many victims tend to have their buttons pushed at the least little thing. Most of the time, they don't have a clue why they act and react the way they do. Their inner wounds need defused! Years of psychiatry rarely help, and pride and ego hinder the process. Only through the renewing of the mind, can man be made whole (Romans 12:2). Every transformation starts in the mind.

Prescription drugs, therapy, and self-help books are only temporary fixes. Inner emotions with deep roots will always push there way back to the surface. It's interesting how the soul lives in a prison of "put downs" and "abuse" long after the abuse is gone. Research has shown that verbal abuse does more emotional damage than physical abuse. Broken homes that leave children separated from one parent or another scars the soul for life, producing feelings of inferiority—not feeling wanted or being good-enough. We all have basic needs to feel worthy and accepted, and when we don't we will find a substitute.

The soul will gravitate towards its comfort-food, and usually in excess. Habits form such as: shopaholic, workaholic, alcoholic, drugs, over-eating, over-spending, sexual perversion, or simply biting finger nails. Rebelling and choosing the wrong side of the law is another avenue. Jails are full of men and women (young & old) who harbor emotional pain—when triggered turn into anger, sometimes uncontrollable rage. Unfortunately no amount of talking (nagging) will help others from sabotaging their lives. Again, it will only come by the renewing of the mind by the Word of God.

When the enemy gets you out of God's presence he can dissuade you out of your purpose, and render you fruitless for a lifetime. Practice God's presence by talking to Him, and reading His WORD daily. If God's Word is void in our lives—life is empty with no real meaning or purpose. When we lean on our own understanding and are living life without knowing God's ways—we become dead branches that are easily combustable.

To be free, the root of the pain must be dealt with. Sometimes the root hibernates so deeply, that a person may not even be aware of it. I was a very happy camper and never once thought I had an issue that needed handling—though as a teenager I told my Grandmother (Gramy), who raised me, that I didn't like my mother. As I look back, it wasn't that I didn't like her; it was because she never gave me the love or attention that I sought. I spoke from a place of hurt and rejection. Years later, after surrendering my life to the Lord, I had an amazing deliverance concerning Mother.

I was visiting my friend Rita Seiffert (Women of the Valley) in Las Vegas. She was leaving for a meeting and was running late. However, as she was going out the door saying good-bye, she quickly turned and said, "I'm supposed to pray for you." She came over to me, got on her knees, and started praying—not knowing what she was to pray about. In minutes she firmly said, "What ever is in there about her mother, come out in the name of Jesus." WOW! It was like the Exorcist—it felt like my head spun completely around! I gasped for breath and started weeping and weeping and weeping, and out of my mouth came the words, "I love my mother." After I was done crying, my weak body got up off the sofa and called her and told her that I loved her. She told me that she loved me too—words that I longed to hear my entire life! That was a major deliverance! My body was so drained that I rested on Rita's sofa for three days after that. That moment in time set me free!

Only the supernatural Power of God can reach into the involuntary workings of the soul. However, if you are aware of the demons that cause you to act out negative behavioral patterns, you can take charge to defuse them. Pray with someone who understands deliverance, or take these issues to God yourself. Talk to Him about those things that are keeping you in bondage. Spending daily quality time with the Lord will lead you out of your particular hell. Start your day with Him, and end your day with Him—always with a grateful heart. The key word is surrender—surrender your life to Jesus!

The one thing that everyone wants is peace of mind. As we live closer and closer to God, inner peace will come. There can be turmoil all around, but we will not be shaken. Philippians 4:7 says, *"And the peace of God, which passeth all understanding, shall keep your hearts and minds through Christ Jesus."* One day I was accused of being "cold" because I didn't get upset about a certain situation. However, I have learned that the calmer a person remains in the middle of a crisis, the faster it will be resolved. When people go ballistic it reveals inner fear. Screaming and throwing things may release built up tensions, but it never cures anything—in fact it only raises the blood pressure. Since fear is the opposite of faith—faith is what is missing.

LET YOUR
FAITH
BE BIGGER
THAN YOUR
FEARS!

As we discussed earlier, it's those old suppressed emotions that cause people to lose it from time to time. The mind, will and emotions must be free of bondages in order to find real joy. If you are in fear of others finding out something that you have been withholding, you are not free. When we are open and above board about everything, that's freedom. Living free starts by loving—look others in the eye with love.

NOTE: Above I stated that screaming is not acceptable; however, when Mel Gibson screamed "FREEDOM" in the 1995 film Braveheart, that scream resonated in my spirit in a way that I will never forget. [If American's wanted FREEDOM as much as that scream cried out for Freedom, we would be looking at a different scenario in the United States today!]

We must intentionally decide to rid ourselves of excess negative baggage, if we don't we will carry it forever. After our "baggage" is unpacked, layer by layer, our suitcase becomes lighter and lighter. Being unencumbered we can now move with a snap in our step. The freer we become, the freer we are to help others remove their heavy loads.

Happiness means different things to different people. Lying on a sunny beach in the Caribbean makes some people happy—others may enjoy sipping hot chocolate in a mountain lodge. If we have a great job…oh happy day! When we are in love…well we know the emotional high that brings! These things are desires of the flesh—and there is nothing wrong with that. Psalms 37:4 says, "Delight thyself also in the Lord; and he shall give thee the desires of thine heart." I encourage you to read Psalms 37 in its entirety.

The happiness for the soul that I am referring to is when we can experience Love, Peace, and Joy regardless of our circumstances. We all have our down times, and sad moments. However, we can be lifted out of them by listening to worship music, praising Jesus, calling a friend, praying, dancing, taking a walk, helping a neighbor, baking cookies, watching a funny movie, listening to an uplifting sermon, reading a book, or we can pull the covers over our head and hide till the feelings pass. What ever works! (Just don't allow yourself to hide too long.) This too shall pass!

Here are three steps to practice if you are down in the dumps. In fact they should be done daily to jump-start your day.

FIRST: Stand up as tall as you can—stomach in, backbone straight. Pretend there is a string attached to your head all the way from heaven. Carry your head high. This is powerful stance that exudes a commanding presence.

SECOND: Think tall mentally! Think winning thoughts. Read this list often and you will take on an inner bigness:

Pray Big! Think Big!
Believe Big! Act Big!
Dream Big! Work Big!
Give Big! Forgive Big!
Laugh Big! Image Big!
Love Big! Live Big!

Most important of all: Think tall spiritually! You are a child of KING JESUS—be loyal to the royal that is in you. Your "crown" has been bought and paid for, all you have to do is put it on—go forth in God's strength ("I can do all things through Christ who strengthens me.").

Take stock of your life and know that life is always in flux and that nothing remains the same forever. Things are either in the process of getting better—or worse. It is up to each individual to decide which direction they want to go. Focus on your purpose—not your problems! If you have a dream in your heart, never give up!

"Get your fire back. It's not over until God says it's over.
Start believing again. Start dreaming again.
Start pursing what God put in your heart."
Dr. Farrah Gray

"Life is like riding a bicycle. To keep your balance you must keep moving."
Albert Einstein
Letter to his son Eduard (Feb. 5, 1930)

Holy Spirit

To be well balanced, I have stressed that the Body needs to be healthy, and the Soul needs to be happy. However, God is more interested in making you (spirit) holy above all else. His main goal for us is to be men and women of integrity and to strive to be more Christ-like. Once you have surrendered your life to *God* and accepted *Jesus* as your *Lord* and *Savior,* is when the greatest adventure of your life begins!

> ♫*Only one life, so soon it will pass,*
>
> *Only what's done for Christ will last.*
>
> *Only one chance to do His will,*
>
> *So give to Jesus all your days.*
>
> *It's the only life that pays.*
>
> *When you recall,*
>
> *You have but one life.*♫[1]

If you are a new Christian you will want to find a church that teaches and preaches Biblical truth. Ask God where He would have you go. A good home-church is a wonderful place to learn and grow, as well as belonging to a prayer group. If you are a seasoned Believer but are stagnant, start talking to God about it—He has a purpose for you to fulfill. If you are baptized in the *Holy Ghost* speak in tongues every-

---

1 Song: *Only One Life* by Lanny Wolfe, Lanny Wolfe Music © 1973

day. Speaking and/or singing in tongues will recharge your spiritual battery. When the gift of tongues is in operation that is the closest we come to experiencing holiness.

Those who are not familiar with what all this "tongue talking" is about may dismiss it from having any importance. Some have even been told it is from the devil. However, I seriously doubt the devil would give people a hunger for God and the gifts of the spirit—which is what happened for me when I received the gift of "tongues." No, you do not have to speak in tongues to be saved or to minister. But it definitely enhances the power of the gospel in our lives (*Acts 1:2*).

Someone once said to me that if I spoke in tongues I would have more power. When hearing this I automatically thought that they were being self-righteous, thinking that they thought they had something I didn't. Fast forward to Bonnie Green's prayer group in Beverly Hills, where Louise French took it upon herself to pray for me week after week to receive tongues. I really didn't know what to think, I would say to her, "I'm open for it if God wants me to have it." Then one fine day while driving home after one of her prayers—up out of my belly and through my mouth came a different language (*Acts 2:4*) I couldn't stop speaking—it was a feeling that was almost euphoric. After that my life took on new meaning: answered prayer, healing miracles, divine encounters, provision and great favor were occurring on a regular basis.

When we are born-again, by the drawing of the *Holy Spirit*, we receive Eternal Life with the *Father*. Then there is an experience whereby we can be filled with the *Holy Ghost* with the evidence of speaking in tongues. Read through the book of Acts—ask the *Holy Spirit* to give you understanding. Pray, asking and believing for *God* to give you this all-powerful gift.

[*The Spirit of the Lord; Spirit of God; Holy Spirit; Holy Ghost* are all different terms for the same spirit—different Bible translations will use one or the other.] The Holy Spirit is the divine source of all life, and special manifestation of God's divine Presence—that part of man that survives death [If you would like a better understanding of the Holy Spirit, I recommend reading *Good Morning Holy Spirit* by Benny Hinn]. When the Presence of God falls on a person it is a tangible feeling. When that anointing is present, is when you will see people healed, delivered, and saved. In God's Presence is where change takes place.

However, Satan can keep you out of God's divine Presence when you let your guard down. Below are 13 evil spirits mentioned by name in the Word of God. These "strong men" must be bound in Jesus name, according *to Matthew 18:18-19* and *Matthew 12:29-30* to deliver the bound and oppressed. These spirits are roaming around looking for a home (body).

1. **Spirit of Bondage:** (*Romans 8:15-16*) Includes all manifestation of compulsory sin, addictions (such as narcotics, alcohol, tobacco, etc.) bad habits. (*Proverbs 5:22*) All controlling spirits work under this "strong man."

2. **Spirit of Fear:** (*11 Timothy 1:7*) We are told in the Bible to "fear not." Fear is not from God. Loose the spirit of faith after binding this strong man of fear.

3. **Dumb & Deaf Spirit:** *Mark 9:25-26* Dumbness (inability to speak) Epilepsy, seizures, suicide, *Mark 9:18-26* Speech impediments, deafness, *Mark 7:32-35, Luke 9:38-39*

4. **Spirit of Heaviness:** *Isaiah 61:3* Abnormal grief, often disguised as a "burden" of intercession—only it never can be prayed thru because it is not a burden but an oppression of the devil. Intense grief, loss of motivation, despair, are characteristic of the attack this spirit brings. Self pity also works with or is brought in by a spirit of heaviness. Loss of joy—*Psalms 69:20.* Condemnation, depression, also work with this spirit. Cure: come to an understanding of forgiveness and redemption (*Ephesians 1:7*). Seek the joy of the Lord!

5. **Spirit of Infirmity:** Often works with spirit of heaviness (*Luke 13-11-13*) which brings in weakness, frailty, chronic illnesses and infections, recurring condition, and is the master spirit behind incurable illnesses.

6. **Spirit of Jealousy:** (*Numbers 5:14*) Brings in spirits of murder, anger, and wrath. Rage and revenge (*Proverbs 6:34*) Causes competitiveness, seeks to destroy unity in homes and churches and in Christian groups of any kind. Brings in hate (*Genesis 37:3-4 & James 3:14-17*). Brings in envying, strife, confusion, suspicion, accusations, and every evil work.

7. **Perverse Spirit:** (*Isaiah 19:14*) Causes deception, misunderstanding of what is said, heard or read. Distorts Word of God or causes it to be heard in a distorted fashion. Causes foolishness for no reason (*Proverbs 12:8*) causes the person to whom it has been assigned to be "lightly esteemed" and ruin reputation and will cause you to fall into mischief (*Proverbs 17:20*).

8. **Spirits of Divination & Familiar Spirits:** *Acts: 16:16-18, 1 Samuel 28:7-9* All occult practices are under this controlling spirit. Seeks to counterfeit the true gifts and manifestations of the *Holy Spirit.*

9. **Spirit of Whoredoms:** *Hosea 4:12* Takes away the heart from God. Backsliding—spirits of apostasy—turning away from God, especially worldly wisdom, things of this world (*James 4:1-4*). Other spirits that work with this one are: adultery, prostitution, child molestation, pornography, fantasy, etc.

10. **Spirit of Haughtiness:** *Proverbs 16:18.* PRIDE— this spirit goes before a fall. It causes one to

overestimate himself and underestimate others. We are to esteem one another higher in love.

11. **Lying Spirit:** *11 Chronicles 18:22* Compulsory lying and exaggeration. Can't help it. This is a bondage!

12. **Spirit of Anti-Christ:** *1 John 4:3* Above all atheism, cults, humanism, and every other "ism" that denies Jesus Christ as the Son of God. Is opposed to any Biblical endeavors.

13. **Unclean Spirit:** *Acts 5:16 & Mark 5:2* The ruler behind mental illnesses. Can demonstrate supernatural strength: causes destruction of the body, mutilation of body, often suicide attempts. Can cause foul odor for no apparent reason, often shows up in a person who is bound by physical uncleanness or dirtiness of living quarters. Can work miracles and gather rulers together for war and destruction (*Revelation 16:13-16*).

If our spirit is messed up everything in our life is messed up. We can be spit and polished on the outside, wearing designer clothes, fine jewelry and a fancy hair-do, but be dirty on the inside!

Plant this in your heart and never forget it:

"Your calling is too high to settle for low living!"

When we become more Christ-like and focus on the Father, Son and Holy Spirit, evil spirits will not have access to our lives. When they try to invade our space, and they will, we need to take authority over them in Jesus name. Sprinkle the blood of Jesus over them and command them to leave. Laugh in the devil's face and kick him out—physically take your foot and kick him. You have the Power and Authority in Jesus name to take charge over every challenge. The salvation of your family, your provision (finances), health issues, what ever your need—speak it in to being and know it is a done deal! See yourself with a backbone of steel! Help your wimpy Christian friends to POWER-UP! When an attack comes, immediately decide not to take it any more, say, "This does not belong to me, you must go in Jesus name."

NOTE: As long as we are willing to live in a frustrated state, the devil will keep dishing it out!

Know your AUTHORITY to speak in the name of Jesus and know that all spirits from the dark-side are compelled to obey you. Pray this simple prayer in your own words.

"I command every spirit of_____ (name them, rejection. fear, guilt, etc.) to go now, and never return, in the name of Jesus of Nazareth."

When I got a hold of the following scripture, actually I should say when this scripture got a hold of me, it changed me spiritually! Meditate on Romans 8:11 (paraphrased): The same spirit that raised Jesus from the dead dwells in me, sending His life through my veins bringing healing through-out my body. THE—SAME—SPIRIT—THAT—RAISED—

JESUS—FROM—THE—DEAD—DWELLS—IN—ME!
Think about that! Is that awesome or what? It's time we
understand the miraculous (Holy) spirit we are carrying!

"The Father says today that your spirit is my house and I
want you to be familiar with my environment within where
I have chosen as My seat of government in the earth. Your
spirit—your human spirit never sleeps and it never slum-
bers. It is always out there working on the areas of need in
your life by My plan and My purpose. Never allow yourself
to have an empty house for your inner man is a coveted
piece of real estate in the realm of the unseen. I so coveted to
make my home in you that I sent My only begotten Son to
make it possible. Your spirit man says the Father is My point
of entry in to your life. Guard your heart and guard your
spirit not allowing anything to enter your spirit through the
mind or emotions that would contaminate or corrupt My
throne room on the inside of you."[2]

NOTE: Holy, Holy, Holy is our God!

---

2 Father's Heart Ministry, Prophets Russ and Kitty Walden. The Daily
Prophetic Word: The Father Says Today January 21, 2015

Notes

7 Days to Greatness Game Plan

"The only thing worse than being blind is having sight but no vision."

Helen Keller

To start your "7 day game plan" pick a day that you can be alone so that you will be able to focus. Starting on a Monday will have you finishing on Sunday. However, your schedule will dictate the start-day that is best for you. Take each days assignment seriously, even if you don't think some of the steps are necessary. This seven day exercise will jump start you to a higher level of living. Goal setting lends itself to a more satisfied life. If you want to know what "freedom" feels like—just do it!

Day 1: Stop everything on this first day and be alone. Pray and meditate freeing your mind of worries and pending problems. When you are relaxed start to look at your past and decide that it will be the last time you are going to dwell on any negative past "stuff"—hang on to the good memories.

With paper in hand, make a list of all past hurts and disappointments—also any anger or unforgiveness issues. After pondering this for a good amount of time (preferably most of the day)—talk to God about it. Give that list to God and then rip it up or burn it. If these old memories continue to haunt you keep giving them to God, every time they surface, until they have no relevance. In some cases it could take weeks. Keep on seeing yourself free and unencumbered.

Now start another list. This time you will think of people that you need to forgive, or those you may owe a letter or phone call to, any unfinished business. It could be as simple as a missed birthday you need to acknowledge. You will be handling that list tomorrow.

NOTE: Your best days lie ahead!

Day 2: When you awake get excited about your second day to freedom. If you are hesitant about today's assignment, pray about it—pray for guidance and wisdom for dealing with your list. Prepare your heart, start by saying Good-Morning to Daddy God and the Holy Spirit.

This is a monumental day—in fact one of the most important! The act of "taking care of unfinished business" will give you a sense of accomplishment as well as feeling like a weight has been lifted. Work on your letters and phone calls that you listed yesterday.—go forgive, go make someone happy, pay unpaid bills, what ever you must do to free up your soul. Send a blessing to each one. Being able to confront people positively develops good communication skills.

If your list is long, you will do a little at a time each day until it is completed. Of course this type of list is never finished as it is part of life. The key is to not let the list become overwhelming—take care of things as they arise.

Always TCB (Take Care of Business) with integrity, others are watching.

Day 3: Today you will be listing your goals. Write down everything you would like to accomplish and everything you would like to have—even the silly things. Have fun with this list—no holds barred. Do yourself a favor and make sure your goals stretch you—reach high!

After you have written all you can think of, prioritize the list by importance. The list will change from time to time as your priorities change. This is normal, as we grow and change our desires change. You will end up eliminating some goals and adding others as weeks and months go by. If the list is too long it can be overwhelming. Statistics show that you can't focus on more than 7 items at a time.

Read the list and keep changing and adding throughout the day until it seems just right. Be specific and detailed about the goal(s). Example: I want a new car is too vague— you must describe the color and make of the car and anything else you want the car to be equipped with. This goes for everything on your list. Be specific!

If you are already clear on your goals and hearts desires and are passionate about them, you are ahead of the game. If not ask your self these questions: What, Why, When, Where, and How for each goal.

Day 4: Today set dates—every goal needs a timeline. Set a date for each goal to be completed. It can be by years end or two years down the road, or a few months—it depends on the goal. But always put: BY and the DATE for each goal. Continue to change and reorganize your list until it is feels just right. If it is already a done deal, read it several times today, thinking about the finished goals with enthusiasm.

Carry the list with you, glancing at it often!

Day 5: Today your goals are completed—in your heart and mind. From now on you will envision your goal(s) completed. Be the person you have decided to be. Never say," I am a "struggling" writer, actor, doctor, lawyer, or truck driver. If you do you will always be reaching for the goal instead of attaining it. Also…you cannot raise above how you see yourself, or what you think about yourself.

Say, "I am (I have)_____!"

Fill in the blank.

Know that you are what you say you are. Just because you may not be making a living at your chosen profession, or your desires have not yet manifested, has no relevance.

This goes for all your goals: Losing weight, dental work, studying the Bible, learning a language, buying a new house—what ever your list contains. Get excited in your spirit by seeing the desired goal completed. Adjust your thinking: "As a man/woman thinketh so is he/she." Practice Being! "BE" the person or the goal—"DO" something towards it everyday—soon you will "HAVE IT."

BE—DO—HAVE

Go and buy something that represents the goal(s). Buy a new pen, brief case, clothes, tools, books—make it something that brings the reality of your desires in to focus. Take a picture of something you want and put it in view where you will see it everyday. Read your list several times today and think of it as often as possible.

Do not talk to anyone about your "plan"—let it come to fruition first.

Day 6: This is the day that the Lord has made, I will rejoice and be glad in it. Speak or sing this until you go into your "happy dance." This is a good way to start everyday, especially if you tend to be groggy or depressed in the morning. Inner joy will help you be excited about your list. The more you feel the joy concerning your hearts desires the more real they become.

If you have given these goals/desires to God and are trusting him completely for the outcome—they have already materialized in the spirit realm. Praise Him for their appearing in the physical realm.

Don't leave home without your list unless you have it memorized.

Day 7: It's celebration day! Your "goals" are in centripetal motion!

Be thankful and "Praise the Lord!"

Wake up Monday morning, or what ever day it is after your seventh day, and continue with your list as you go about your day. If you feel like repeating the last seven days once again—do it! Refer to your list often (at least three times a day) and think about what you want as often as possible.

Remember: This is between you and God, do not talk to others about your goals.

"Live, Love, Laugh, and Let God Guide Your Path!"
April Shenandoah

Albert Einstein

The only limits that exist are those we put on ourselves! We are definitely puppets to our past emotions; however, we can renew the mind and literally cut the strings from the past.

ASSIGNMENT: Get a piece of paper and draw a puppet. Now add the strings and write every "hurtful memory and pain of your heart" on each string that you want to be free of. After you name your strings, use your imaginary scissors to cut the strings off your puppet, or simply crumble it all up and give it to God. Tell God "thank you" for helping you to renew your mind—thank him for your renewed mind every time negative thoughts start to creep in. Remember, the mind is the devil's playground. Decide that enough is enough! Make the decision to go forward, leaving the past behind.

Use these verbal suggestions when cutting your puppet strings:

1. I cut that out of my life forever—in Jesus name
2. I choose to release this—in Jesus name
3. I erase that memory—in Jesus name
4. I choose to forgive—in Jesus name
5. There is nothing to fear—in Jesus name

I am a child of the living God and I am loved!

If God is for me who can be against me!

With God all things are possible!

"Thank you Lord for renewing my mind!"

The idea is to be free like this little guy.

About the Author

April Shenandoah has gone from Show Business to God's Business, and when the passion strikes—political activist. In 1988, she developed an appetite for politics when she served as the Los Angeles press contact for Pat Robertson's presidential campaign. A few years later, she combined politics and religion on her cable TV show *The Bottom Line*. Her first book *So...Help Me God also delved into politics and religion—she says they are the two things we MUST talk about!

Since 2000, April's column *Politics & Religion* appeared in the *Tolucan Times*. After 10 years of writing about controversial political issues, she is now concentrating on more uplifting subject matter.

April had a lesson in faith that changed her direction, and is now helping others to find their Godly purpose in life. As Ambassador of Prayer, she knows that "Whatever the question—prayer is the answer." Her 3H coaching on the Body (Healthy) Soul (Happy) and Spirit (Holy) sets the captives free. She also teaches on the power of words, as laid out in *Your Tongue Determines Your Destiny*.

For further information about April's books, workshops, or speaking schedule, contact April at:

E-mail: aprilshenandoah@politicsandreligion.tv

E-mail: ambassadorofprayer@gmail.com

Website: aprilshenandoah.com

Phone: 800-997-1717

*So...Help Me God! (Collectible)

The Harrison House Vision

Proclaiming the truth and the power

Of the Gospel of Jesus Christ

With excellence;

Challenging Christians to

Live victoriously,

Grow spiritually,

Know God intimately.

Fast. Easy.
Convenient.

For the latest Harrison House product information and author news, look no further than your computer. All the details on our powerful, life-changing products are just a click away. New releases, E-mail subscriptions, testimonies, monthly specials—find it all in one place. Visit harrisonhouse.com today!

harrisonhouse